George Johnson, Mary Shoemaker Johnson

The Roll-Call

And Other Poems

George Johnson, Mary Shoemaker Johnson

The Roll-Call
And Other Poems

ISBN/EAN: 9783744705486

Printed in Europe, USA, Canada, Australia, Japan

Cover: Foto ©Thomas Meinert / pixelio.de

More available books at **www.hansebooks.com**

AND

OTHER POEMS.

BY

GEORGE JOHNSON.

———

PHILADELPHIA:
J. B. LIPPINCOTT & CO.
1876.

PREFACE.

IT was the intention of my dear husband to have published a little volume of poems appropriate in general to the Centennial, but he being called to the Higher Life before its completion, I have endeavored so far as practicable to carry out his plan concerning it. A number of poems intended especially for this work not having been completed, I have thought best to introduce some of his earlier productions, which I trust will prove acceptable. Hoping the public will be lenient to all errors they may discover, I venture to send it forth.

M. S. J.

BUCKS CO., PA., October, 1875.

CONTENTS.

CONTENTS.

THE ROLL-CALL OF THE OLD THIRTEEN.

I.

A VOICE from a mountain height,
  As sweet as an air in June,
    As solemn as the sea,—
A voice not in the night,
  But the near and naked noon.
    What shall the answer be?
Listen and look and lean,
  Tremble and be afraid,
Answer, Old Thirteen!
  For to you the call is made.

II.

MASSACHUSETTS:

I hear the voice and I know;
  Liberty, can it be said
    I was faithless to thee and to law?
I am here as I was long ago,
  Here with my living and dead.
    Not with an oath and its awe

Would I say I did my best
   In the service of freedom and truth;
But look at the scars on my breast
   And the hope in the hearts of my youth!

III.

NEW HAMPSHIRE:

Show me thy glorious face,
   Goddess that callest to me.
     Sweet spirit! let me be cheered—
But no,—in the freedom-blessed race
    Whose homes on my granite are reared,
   Thy features reflected I see.
"Here!" is my answer for them
   When Right for their service shall call;
The flood of the fight they would stem
   Till slaughter had swallowed them all.

IV.

CONNECTICUT:

Here, with the flag of thy stars,
   The red and the white and the blue,
    Held in my hand and my heart,
   Stricken with shot through and through.
    To shield it I did my part

When thunder and battle-blast
  Swept round it like prairie flame;
But what is past is past,—
  The glory is more than the shame.

v.

RHODE ISLAND:

They smile at me since I am least,
  But the burden I share with the whole.
    If I honor the work that I do
Am I worthy to sit at the feast
    With the rich and the great,—since the true
  Stature of man is the soul?
I heard the wail and the call
  Of the perishing land in her woes;
I gave her my little, my all;
  Perhaps 'twas that saved her,—who knows?

vi.

NEW YORK:

If empire chiefly I sought,
  Prosperity, honors, and ease,
    Surely it cannot be said
After the years I have wrought,
    I languish for lack of these,
      Or for promise of power ahead.

Loyal and loving I stand ;
    And were I queen of the earth,
What, I would ask, is a land
    Without order and liberty worth?

VII.

PENNSYLVANIA :

As after the storm-cloud's march,
    Broad in the beamy blue,
        Iris spans valley and hill,
So shines the ocean-shored arch,
    Built in the world's wide view,
        And I am its keystone still.
Green are my heart and my hills,
    And as fresh as the water that runs
In the mossy pipes of my rills
    Are the fervor and faith of my sons.

VIII.

NEW JERSEY :

Still on my soil are the stains
    That were left by patriots' feet,
        Sore after battle and rout ;
Not all the century's rains,
    Not all the snows that have beat,
        Have washed them entirely out.

Elsewhere 'neath battle-trod earth
  Count I the graves of my lost.
Know I not liberty's worth,
  Purchased at such a cost?

IX.

MARYLAND:

Blandished and tempted and torn,
  Caught in the whirlwind of war,
    In the mazes of dreams that were lies,
A light that was not of the morn
  Flashed from a perilous shore,
    Blazed on and blinded mine eyes.
Like a star on heaven's blue brink,
  I was ready to chaos to fall;
I wavered, but did not sink,—
  Thank God! I can answer the call.

X.

DELAWARE:

With the terrible tread of War
  The continent shaking I heard,
    In the shadow of thunder I lay
Watching the fight from afar.
  At last a song like a bird!
    At last a light like a star!

Then I opened my eyes on the war;
  The red lightnings paused in their play,
And brighter than ever before
  Shone the promise of permanent day.

XI.

VIRGINIA:

I stand not where once I stood.
  Scathe me in annal and verse,
    Tell my whole story of shame:
Say that I bargained in blood,
  Was kind to a palpable curse,—
    Where is my once white name?
But something comes up with the tide,
  Wide blown as the breaths of the sea,—
A newer and better pride
  That hints of a glory to be.

XII.

NORTH CAROLINA:

Goddess, what have I to show
  As harvest of rich years of time?
    Here liberty early abode;
I promised thee fair long ago,
  But I shared in the popular crime,
    And later I reaped as I sowed.

But give me a place in the line,
　The years of the future are long ;
I will walk in the light of the sign,—
　Of the sign of the sinking of wrong.

XIII.

SOUTH CAROLINA :

Vanquished, but guilty no less,
　Bowing my heart and my head,
　　Here am I, ashamed in the light ;
Saved from disastrous success,
　Ghosts of armies of dead
　　Haunt me by day and by night.
And yet what I did I did ;
　As ye will interpret my tears.
Can the shame of a crime be hid
　After a thousand years ?

XIV.

GEORGIA ·:

Am I last to answer the call ?
　Here, by my sister's side,
　　I ask, is there pardon for me ?
Had we compassed the Union's fall
　'Twere well with my dead to have died,
　　Or that I were sunk in the sea.

But the tempest of battle is o'er,
The sky shows its blue serene,
And we count in the heavens once more
The stars of the Old Thirteen !

ODE.

FOR JULY 4TH, 1876.

I.

IT comes ! the expected day,
Blissful in every ray.
Put all annoy
And selfish care away.
The summer land lies fair,
Nature with us doth share
The general joy.

II.

A hundred years have gone
Since freedom's cloudy dawn
Burst into day ;
Its sun is rolling on
Through free, rejoicing skies,
And in our joy we rise
As free as they !

III.

Cities and peaceful farms!
Th' occasion's sweet alarms
  Your rest shall break;
'Tis no wild call to arms;
To hail with patriot pride
This glad centennial tide,
  Awake! awake!

IV.

Ye mountains, stand and be
Types of the liberty
  That now is ours;
As firmly stand may we.
Ye prairies, glad and green,
Toss in your varied sheen,
  Like seas of flowers!

V.

Rejoice, ye conscious trees!
Concordant with the breeze,
  Your branches wide
Wave in its airy seas.
Old Ocean, roll and roar
The green length of your shore
  In solemn pride.

VI.

Rivers! rejoicing run,
Like silver in the sun,
    Ye sea-like deeps!
The anthem is begun;
A murmur like the main
Add to the growing strain
    That o'er you sweeps!

VII.

The banners, bright as bloom,—
The thunder, boom on boom,—
    The festal fires
That shall the street illume,
Blazing as if they knew
Their glare prolongs the view,
    As day expires,—

VIII.

The steeple's lifted bell,—
Music's exultant swell,—
    The clang and call,—
The people's joy these tell;
But note not it alone,—
A solemn undertone
    Runs through it all.

IX.

They feel—they deeply feel
Their country's woe and weal
    Dates fresh to-day,
As reverently they kneel
To take the mighty trust
Which Thou, Great Sovereign, dost
    Upon them lay.

X.

God of the nations, Thou
To whom all earth doth bow,
    Where shall we stand
A hundred years from now?
A thousand?—Old as Rome,
Will Freedom still her home
    Have in our land?

XI.

Teach us, teach us to be
As worthy to be free
    As were our sires;
Then shall the future see,
Burning on all our heights,
Freedom's unlessened lights
    And virginal fires!

AMERICA TO ENGLAND ON THE OCCASION OF THE CENTENNIAL, 1876.

WELCOME to thee, our mother-guest!
  The child advanced to manhood's claim,
Though parted from the parent breast
  Knows whence it came.

The tie of blood is close and strong,
  We cannot break it if we would.
'Kin knoweth kin, though oft and long
  Misunderstood.

We once were foes, but better days
  Dawn o'er the darkness and the ill.
We loved thee once; and, to our praise,
  We love thee still.

Dear mother-country! yes, oh, yes,
  It is thy child that to thee speaks,
A good will striving to express,
  Like that it seeks.

Though 'tween us, stormy, dark, and wide,
  The waters of an ocean run,
Who shall our histories divide?
  The two are one!

Our English tongue,—it is a sign
  That shows how close we are to thee.
Our rise was thine, our progress thine,
  Our fall would be.

We share thy glory and thy shame,
  All thou hast lost, all thou hast won;
With knightly Sidney's twine the name
  Of Washington.

So through the long illustrious list
  Of names wide given to renown,
Laurels with laurels intertwist
  From Chaucer down.

Great Shakspeare's fame and Runnymede,—
  We think of these as half our own,—
And Cromwell, whose red, daring deed
  Smote king and throne.

Art thou unwilling we should claim
  So large a portion of thy past?
If then thy own, our final fame
  Grows even more vast.

3

Time will remember whence we bring
 The strength that gathers like a sea,
And proudly will its parent spring
 Be traced to thee.

Freedom and love of freedom—both
 Came to us from thine own estate.
And now our hundred years of growth
 We celebrate.

An honored guest, behold the land
 Nature and God so amply bless,
The elements of empire grand
 That we possess.

Our institutions, systems, aims,
 All that we are or hope to be,
To worth their weak or powerful claims
 Come close to see.

Behold us ! and with kindly eyes,
 Forgiving faults thou canst but mark ;
Too long our mutual sympathies
 Have lain in dark.

That we have passed the unjust sneer
 Upon each other each will own ;
Bold censure, glad to be severe,
 We both have known.

The critic's is a dangerous art,
　　And when it prides itself to pain
And raise a rancor in the heart,
　　Whose is the gain ?

Nations—great nations, too—may be
　　As petty as the private mind,
To hate and groundless jealousy
　　Meanly inclined.

Our lower instincts scorning then,
　　As Christian nations let us act,
Till "Peace on earth, good will to men"
　　Become a fact.

1776.　INDEPENDENCE HALL.　1876.

AN ODE FOR THE CENTENNIAL.

I.

OLD HALL, we give thee greeting
　　From continent and isle ;
The centuries are meeting
　　Above thine honored pile.
　　　Broad to the skies
　　　Our glad land lies,
　　Basking in Freedom's smile.

II.

What memories throng upon us,
  Richer than Runnymede !
A hundred years have shown us
  The value of the seed
    Our fathers sowed
    In tears and blood,—
  Ay, Time approves the deed.

III.

That glorious Declaration,
  Old Hall, from thee went forth ;
Within thy walls the nation
  Had its triumphant birth.
    No place to fame
    Has greater claim,
  Thou classic spot of earth !

IV.

Long, long within the steeple
  The bell had silent hung ;
Below, the waiting people
  Listened to hear its tongue.
    Hark ! ne'er before
    On any shore
  So glad a peal was rung !

v.

The summer-vault of heaven
  Could not contain the sound,
The continents were riven
  To their remotest bound.
    'Twas not alone
    The Bell's glad tone,—
  God's voice was in the sound !

vi.

Dead as the dust of Edom
  Old nations long had lain ;
That mighty peal of freedom
  Roused them to life again.
    From living graves,
    No longer slaves,
  They rose once more to reign !

vii.

"Men are created equal ;"
  'Twas a simple thing to say,
But a dark and bloody sequel
  Was dated from that day,
    When infant right
    And giant might
  Engaged in desperate fray. ·

3*

VIII.

The end was greater glory
   Than the sword has often won.
We know the starry story
   Of what was dared and done ;
     And thou, old Hall,
     Dost best recall
The dawn of Freedom's sun.

IX.

Those beams of blessing on us
   A hundred years have shone ;
The rights our fathers won us,
   Secure, are still our own.
     My land ! arise
     And recognize
The favors thou hast known !

X.

Grateful and glad thy voicing
   By every hearth should fall ;
But centre thy rejoicing
   Around the grand old Hall.
     Welcome them here
     From far and near,
The friendly nations all.

XI.

Fling out the flag and pennon,
　The festal scene to grace ;
Let the unshotted cannon
　Thunder its solemn bass,
　　While band and bell
　　The rapture swell,
　And joy lights every face.

XII.

Let Industry, displaying
　Her varied triumphs, stand
Crowned in our midst, surveying
　Her good work in the land,—
　　Her rich increase,
　　While Power and Peace
　Attend her, hand in hand.

XIII.

Glad sight ! Old Hall, repeated
　May it for ages be,
Unless, of Freedom cheated,
　We fall, perhaps ere thee.
　　No, no ; our land
　　Still strong must stand,
　An Empire of the Free !

XIV.

Yet Freedom's favor waneth
　Where greed takes foremost place;
As sovereign she reigneth
　With an exacting grace;
　　She will not stay
　　Where men decay,
　But loves a virtuous race.

SONG.

WRITTEN FOR THE OCCASION OF THE CELEBRATION OF
THE ONE HUNDREDTH ANNIVERSARY OF THE BOSTON
TEA-PARTY.

SAID royal George, "My subjects thrive,
　My subjects o'er the sea;
Cannot my ministers contrive
　Their thrift shall prosper me?
Few men drink wine, but all drink tea,—
　A tax on it I'll lay;
For our good úse none will refuse
　So small a sum to pay."
And soon in fact the royal act
　Was sent across the sea;
So, Betty, fill the kettle up,
　We'll all take tea.

But, sooth to say, the king's desire
    Did not approval find;
His free-born subjects rose in ire
    And plainly spoke their mind:
"If prince or peer tax what we drink
    And never ask our leave,
Then what we eat, we can but think,
    Will next their care receive."
Cold and black shall hang the rack,
    The urn shall empty be;
So, Betty, take the kettle off,
    We won't drink tea.

All royal England could not stir
    The people from their way;
Tea-parties grew unpopular,
    Save one—in Boston Bay!
Oh, matchless men were those of yore!
    As chainless as the sea,
And every cup to-night we pour
    Shall in their honor be.
The tyrant's yoke for us they broke,—
    The cup we drink is free;
So, Betty, fill the kettle up,
    We'll all drink tea.

THE VOICES OF THE CLOCKS.

I.

From parlor and hall
I heard the clocks call,—
  The new and the old.
The hour, lone and late,
  By both was just told.
    Within was soft light
From the low-burning grate;
    Outside was the night
And the iron-like cold.

II.

No star dared to wink;
No sound save the clink
  Now and then of a coal;
    No footstep, nor stir;
The house held its breath,
  And over me stole
A sense as of death,—
Of a presence to which
    All life did defer,

And whose shadow o'ercast
  My soul with a pall,
As if I and the vast
  Lonely darkness were all.

III.

Then the clocks each to each,
In unusual speech,
  Called through the dim air.
With a stern, stately stroke
The old clock first spoke
  From its niche on the stair.
  I pictured it there,
Like a monk cloaked and tall,
  With its great, grave face
  And the coffin-like case,
Standing straight 'gainst the wall.

  "Alas! alas!" it said,
  "The best of life has fled,
  The dear old days are dead,
      And come no more.
  Mournful I keep my trust,
  The bloom has died to dust,
  The red has changed to rust,
      So bright before.

"'Time's weary sentinel,
Long have I stood to tell
The household 'All is well,'
        With Time at least.
Often my mournful stroke
The funeral silence broke;
Again it gladly spoke
        The wedding feast.

"But in this mansion proud,
My tick once clear and loud,
(How fast the moments crowd
        It to the worst!)
After so many years
Sounds like the fall of tears,—
Alas! where are the ears
        That heard it first?

"Oh, generations dead!
Oh, forms and faces fled!
How full has death been fed
        On your decay!
And what remaineth now?
The silence and the snow,—
But tell me, who art thou
        That seem'st so gay?"

A chime rang silvery low.
Above the marbly glow
(Like rose-light upon snow)
    A face was seen.
The ormolu shone bright,
The costly malachite
Flashed back a mingled light
    Of gold and green.

The bronze deer stood in grace
A-top the ebony case;
An almost human face
    Beamed tranquil there,
By marble darkness bound.
Again that silvery sound
Plashed in the lake-like round
    Of the still air.

It said: " How sad thy tone,
Old friend, that there alone
Dost stand and make thy moan !
    My tuneful tongue
Shall cheer this sombre room ;
This firelight shines like bloom ;
I do not feel the gloom."
    " No ; thou art young."

" Dark lies the frost-locked ground,
But through the blue profound
The sun doth keep his round ;
    His golden keys
Shall ope the earth again
To the renewing. rain,
Why, then, dost thou complain
    Of hours like these?"

" 'Tis not," the sad voice said,
" Because the spring is dead,
And summer's sweetness fled,
    I sorrow so ;
Nature I still can trust ;
The dead rose from the dust
Will rise again, and must,
    When June airs blow.

" But there are sadder things
Than wasting winter brings,—
A chill that deeper stings
    Than white-fanged frost.
Sweet rains from warm clouds poured
Shall green again the sward,
But when shall be restored
    What Love has lost?

"For me this very night
A century ends its flight,
And thoughts come like a blight
    My spirit o'er;
For, thinking of the past,
I see, as if forecast,
The future, vague and vast,
    Gloom up before."

"The future!" raptly cried
The young voice at my side;
"*I* hail its coming tide,
    Its rising roar.
Clouds it will bring, I know,
But, like their billowy flow
In spring, when south winds blow,
    How rich its store!

"Above its shadowy drift
The peaks of promise lift,
With here a rosy rift
    And there a blue."
The voice spoke from the stair:
"Oh, thou dost paint it fair,
But long it cannot wear
    Such heavenly hue."

The other, in reply,
Said : " Must I, then, deny
The beauty I descry ?
  Must I, like thee,
Forego the prospect fair ?
Shape the delicious air
To tempest-beatings, where
  Mad ruin shall be ?"

The answer was : " No, no ;
Thou need'st not think it so.
I only sought to show
  The temperate truth.
This earthly life of ours
Is not made up of flowers,
Of sunny scenes and hours,
  Of warmth and youth.

" At first so fair it seems,
The young heart dreams and dreams,
But wakes to find the beams
  It loved withdrawn.
Blight falleth on the bloom,
The air, once all perfume,
Grows thick with thunderous gloom,
  And age steals on."

Then said, in saddened tone,
The other: " Thou hast grown
Old at the post, and known
    All this to be.
If all our hopes are lies,
If evening her tired eyes
Must always close with sighs
    On misery;

"Surely it then were best
For all things to have rest,
Close sunken on earth's breast,
    No more to rise.
Why should the roses bloom,
If but across the tomb
To waft their lost perfume
    'Neath mocking skies?"

" Forgive my mournful mood.
More lightly than I should,"
The old clock said, "the good
    Of life I scan.
Let me destroy no cheer,
But ever hold more dear
The spirit needed here
    So much by man:

4*

"A patient heart to wait,
Ready for any fate,
With gladness not too great,
    Nor too subdued.
Doing life's earnest work,
Too brave to pause or shirk,
Whether the skies be murk
    Or rosy-hued."

I.

Then merrily through the listening air,
From the mantel and the stair,
    Called the clocks together.
The gaining day leaned toward the light,
Faint star-points pierced the pall of night,
The inside cheer soon put to flight
    The thoughts of winter weather.

II.

Half dreaming that I had not dreamed,
So real had the voices seemed,
    I rose and crossed the hall-way.
Each pendulum-pulse in concord beat,
Sad age had felt youth's influence sweet,
And cooled in turn the latter's heat;
    And so it should be alway.

December 15, 1874.

AT WASHINGTON'S CROSSING.

O'ER the river brightly flowing,
  O'er the green-shored Delaware,
And the landscape golden-glowing,
  Swept the warm, wide waves of air.

'Twas the teeming time of summer;
  All the land was full of cheer,
Wind and stream in mingled murmur
  Poured their cool sound on my ear.

By an old oak shut and shaded
  From the vast exterior day,
All the present from me faded
  As upon that shore I lay.

'Twas a classic shore, for yonder,
  Just across the bright blue tide,
Where the heavy train in thunder
  Rushes by the valley's side,

Once a little patriot army
  Pressed with painful, eager tramp,
Through the freezing night and stormy,
  Toward the sleeping Hessian camp.

Aye, a scene rose up before me,
  Darkly changed from this of light,—
Not the summer noon was o'er me,
  But the frigid winter night.

To essay the perilous crossing
  Gathered here that hero band.
'Mid the ice their frail boats, tossing,
  Struggle for the hostile land.

Oh, the toil, the cold, the danger!
  Freemen, do you think of these?
Do you e'er in fancy change your
  Homes of peace and beds of ease

For the dark and frowning river?
  For the sore march and the fray?
For the cold whose icy quiver
  Cuts the glow of life away?

The remembrance fondly cherish
  Of the men none could enslave,
For a nation can but perish
  That forgets its good and brave.

SONG: THE OLD-FASHIONED FIRE-PLACE.

I.

THE old, old-fashioned fireplace!
  Ah! it has had its day,
And the old, old-fashioned dwellers,
  They, too, have passed away.
No more the wood-fire flashes
  The country hearth upon,—
Ashes, ashes, ashes!
  The past is dead and gone.
But something of its mettle
  Is welded with our lives;
And the singing of the kettle
  Its memory revives.

II.

We see the homely grouping
  Around the settler's hearth:
The grandsire gray and stooping,
  And almost done with earth;
The grandma at her knitting,
  The children strong and tall,

And flitting, flitting, flitting
  Against the chimney-wall,
The glow that lights their faces,—
  The pure, fresh, living flame,—
Oh ! it was from such places
  The strength of freedom came !

III.

The old, old-fashioned fireplace !
  We have no need to-day
To build its wide volcanic top
  To give our hearth-fires play.
But we have need still longer
  Our sires to emulate,
Stronger, stronger, stronger
  To build both home and state.
With all that we inherit,
  That the fruitful present bears,
Say, can we show a spirit
  That can fully match with theirs ?

IV.

The old, old-fashioned fireplace !
  It was a roaring sight
To see the sparks like fire-flies
  Shoot upward through the night.

If Winter, the old stormer,
　　Raised a louder din,
Warmer, warmer, warmer
　　Glowed the hearts within.
Young hope and faith and fervor !
　　Oh ! these lift up a land,
And well her sons will serve her
　　If these she can command.

v.

The old, old-fashioned fireplace !
　　We seem to feel its blaze
Burn through the vanished winters
　　And light our later days.
Oh, cheeks so bright and blushing !
　　Your bloom has done away ;
But we feel your warm blood rushing
　　Along our veins to-day.
The grateful heart remembers
　　What idle hearts forget ;
We feel the glorious embers
　　Of the past are living yet.

SONG OF THE CITY.

Oh, the heart with its merciless beat !
   And its rivers of red that run !
Oh, the brain with its haste and heat !
   I am heart and brain in one.
As the waves of mind's mystical sea
   Flow ever from pole to pole,
So the currents of life in me,
   For I am its centre and soul.

When earth for the first was green
   In the eyes of the children of men,
They gave me the title of Queen,
   And mine it has been since then.
Mine, with few to divide
   The honors of empire with me,
For my rule as the earth is as wide,
   My strength as the strength of the sea.

The tramp of the train on the shore,
   The tremble and trill of the wire,
The pant of the piston, the roar
   Of furnace and forge all a-fire,

The smoke-drift afloat on the air,
  The shimmer of sails on the sea,—
What are they but signs that declare
  The world is still toiling for me?

The mountains with riches are stored,
  The soil with its harvests,—for me
Their tribute and treasure are poured,
  As rivers are poured to the sea.
In my close and passionate life
  I dream, and I dream of peace,
Yet I grow more in love with a strife
  That I know can never cease.

The sounds of my splendid unrest
  They woo with a magical power,
And I gather the brightest and best
  Around me to flourish and flower,—
And to fall, you may say. Ah! yes;
  Alas for the souls that go down,
The brave and the brilliant no less
  Than the thousands unasking renown!

5

SONG OF THE TELEGRAPH.

MEN praised in the long ago
    That fiery courser, the Sun ;
Now his golden car is slow
    And Time itself outrun.

For the live electric fire,
    Behold ! is tamed and taught ;
On my trilling tracks of wire
    It flies with the speed of thought.

Steam is a panting hack,
    Toiling with fettered heels ;
I flit to his goal and back
    In a single roll of his wheels.

Farewell to the lagging breeze !
    In the calms of night it drops,
While, flashing under the seas
    And over the mountain-tops,

My starry words I wing
    Along the nerve-like wire,
That thrills like a conscious thing
    To my flying touch of fire.

Zone unto zone I bind,
    · Tropic to polar shore ;
And the nations shout to find
    That distance is no more.

From me the soul a hint
    Receives of its future powers,
As the dawning's sanguine glint
    Foretells noon's riper hours.

I am the wildest dream
    That ever to fact was wrought ;
In me a closer gleam
    Of the infinite is caught.

My glory and renown
    An age triumphant sings,—
I am the star and crown
    Of brain-created things.

Yet not the lowly grass
    Nor the humbler dust I scorn,
For I know the mighty mass
    Of the universe was born

Each part with an equal claim
    To the thoughtful mind's regard :

No more my subtle flame
    Than the rock so dull and hard.

There is a mystic tie
    That doth all things unite :
The soul that cannot die
    With those of sense and sight.

The skies that o'er earth span
    Are kin to her own green sod.
There's divinity in man
    And humanity in God !

THE SLAVE AUCTION-BELL.

(In the town of Beaufort, North Carolina, a large bell that before the war was used to call buyers to slave auctions was afterwards hung in a building occupied by a colored school, and employed to call the children to their studies.)

In the town the bell was hung,
    And it rung
From its iron lips, year by year,
Not a peaceful call to prayer
    On the air,
For the worshipful to hear ;

Not a clamorous peal of war,
Telling that to waste their shore
    Came some foeman bold,
But a call that terror gave
Only to the shackled slave,
    Waiting to be sold.

To the poor slave-mother's breast
    Closer pressed
Was her trembling child in fear,
As that bell with heavy stroke
    Harshly spoke
That the parting hour was near.
Lowly bosoms heaved with sighs,
Eyes looked sadly into eyes
    Nevermore to meet again,
As that sad sound, ringing high,
Wronged the free, rejoicing sky,
And the people came to buy—
    Buy their fellow-men !

Error cannot always last;
    Battle-blast
Swept the hoary curse away.
There's a gladder tale to tell, —
    Hear the bell
As it rings and swings to-day:

" Ye, who once like beasts were bought,
Come as freemen to be taught.   *
From your long, dark ignorance
In the blessed light advance
    Of the school.
Right has triumphed, Right is strong,
And the iron hand of Wrong
    Cannot rule."

Thus with fine poetic force
    Does the course
Of great evil sometimes end.
Sometimes from the very stones
Freedom's sweet-awakened tones
    Do ascend.
Masters! tyrants! mark it well,—
    In some hour
Voices wherewith you proclaim
Your defenseless fellows' shame,
May in turn pronounce the knell
    Of your power!

THE CENTENARIAN.

HE sits by his Northern hearth to-day,
 Far from the noise of the red frontiers ;
An old, old man whose few locks are gray
 With the frosts of a hundred years.
His aged face is wrinkled and wan,
 And the blood in his veins is thin and cold,
But his soul is that of the strong, brave man,
 And his heart is not yet old.

Ere the land that we now bless as our own
 Took its place 'mid the nations of earth,
And our beautiful flag to the wind was thrown,
 He had his wildwood birth.
From the humble door of the pioneer
 He first looked up to the smiling sun,
And the first loud sound that fell on his ear
 Was the crack of the hunter's gun.

Oh ! a ruder cradle you seldom will see
 Than that which was rocked by the settler's fire,
And never a bolder lad than he,—
 The son of the settler sire !

His hair was like night, his cheek like morn,
　His form like his father's, straight and tall,
And his voice as mellow as that of the horn
　Sounding the hunter's call.

To him oft, when the blast howled through the trees
　And the chimney wall was ruddy with flame,
Had the tale been told, how over the seas
　The Pilgrim Fathers came.
And many another tale he had learned
　Of what men for freedom's sweet sake will do,
Till deep in his bosom's core there burned
　A hate for the tyrant crew.

"Oh, pa!" asked the boy once when he had mused
　O'er a story of people who filled bondmen's graves,
"Do you think like *them* we'll ever be used,—
　Oh, pa! will *we* ever be slaves?
You say that our rulers grow crueler each day
　And will not be warned; will they crush us?" he said.
"Ah, boy!" spoke the sire as he put him away,
　"I fear there are storms ahead."

And soon did the tempest-cloud blacken the air,
　And wider and fiercer it swept on its path;
The people had borne all that freemen could bear,
　And now they arose in their wrath.

They spurned and they trampled the English laws,
  And felt it a better and nobler thing
To fight and to fall in Liberty's cause
  Than cringe to the English king.

And the young lad heard the proud news told
  Of Lexington's long-remembered fray,
Ere the blood of the slain was scarce yet cold
  And the deed but yesterday.
Then wilder the tap of the rallying drum
  Rolled over the arming, desperate land,
And he saw in hot haste from the furrow come
  Brave Putnam and his band.

They called to his father as by him they spurred,
  Who turned from the work he had just begun—
His soul all on fire with the tidings he heard—
  And went to the house for his gun.
Then the boy smothered down his few faint fears,
  And eagerly asked if *he* might go
Along with the rest of the volunteers
  And fight the British foe.

But the father only proudly smiled
  As he gazed in those eyes so clearly blue,
Kissed warmer the lips of his wife and child,
  And bade them both adieu;

Then northward marched to share the renown
  .Of Ticonderoga's deed of fame,
Where the flag of the British fort came down
  "In the great Jehovah's name!"

In a score of fights he took full part
  As those terrible years of strife wore on,
Then a bullet was sent to the patriot's heart,
  And the patriot's life was gone.
Then the boy, who was now a strong youth grown,
  Wiped the tear-drops hot from his mother's face,
Took the dead one's rifle and cloak as his own,
  And stood in the father's place.

At Yorktown he toiled in the grim redoubt,
  Where the shot and the shell in fury poured,
Till he saw O'Hara march humbly out
  And give up his chieftain's sword.
Then the stars of peace, with a holy flush,
  To the thunder-filled sky the soldier saw come,
And the foe, from the men they could not crush,
  Slunk back to their island home.

Oh, then was the long, long woe repaid!
  The oppressor's might could not prevail;
The right and the wrong God's hand had weighed;
  And the right had turned the scale!

Oh ! grandly the breast of the youth would heave
  As he thought of that glorious victory-hour,
And trod the soil he had helped retrieve
  From the haughty despot's power !

The years rolled on, till across the main
  The host of the Briton came once more,
When he shouldered his musket and hurried again
  To strike for his native shore.
On Niagara's field and at Chippewa
  He saw the lines of the red-coats break,
And with Macomb gallantly fought one day
  At Plattsburg by the lake.

The enemy, humbled on plain and tide,
  Their sails soon set to the western breeze,
And, broken once more in their strength and pride,
  Sped over the distant seas.
The years rolled on, and star after star
  Blazed out on our banner's azure hue,
Till the State that was born 'mid the thunders of war
  To a mighty nation grew.

Still the old man lived, though one by one
  His comrades, hoary and honored and blessed,
Drew their hands away from their labors done,
  And went to their happy rest.

Still the old man lived; till the traitor's blade
  Struck deep at the nation's honor and life,
And the armies of treason against us arrayed
  Rushed on to the dreadful strife.

And now, as he thinks of these stormy days,
  A shade, as of doubt, oft crosses his brow;
But he smiles it away, and often says
  'Tis grand to be living now.
He mourns for the dear lives daily lost,
  For the desolate homes and the bitter woe,
But he feels that the prize is worth the cost,
  Fearful it be although.

As sure as the sunshine follows the rain,
  And stars shine out from their depths of blue,
He says that our country will stand strong again
  If *we* are watchful and true.
And he often prays, if it only might be
  That the lamp of his life may not go out
Till Peace has smiled on us, and *he* lived to see
  The end of this trouble and doubt.

November, 1864.

THE STORY OF THE PINE.

THE fairest of the forest forms,
  The loftiest of its line,
The loudest of the winter's storms,
  Thus spoke the ancient Pine:

" When first I reared my infant head
  Cannot with truth be told,
But often have I heard it said
  I am a century old.

" And surely since upon the beach
  I broke the emerald moss,
The changes I have seen would reach
  A hundred years across.

" Never the lightning-stroke has rent
  My boughs nor scorched my grain;
And kindly Heaven has always sent
  The dew and vital rain.

"Oh, oft with joy have I the fierce
  And flashing tempest met,

6

Or felt my strong roots slowly pierce
 The dark earth deeper yet.

"For does all conscious joy belong
 To human forms alone?
Have I not senses fine and strong,
 Perhaps, as are your own?

"Am I a dull, unknowing thing,
 When 'neath the uncovered sky
I feel the tingling tides of spring
 Within me mounting high?

"Or when my branches, shower-wet,
 The sudden sunlight strikes,
Or when the winter rain has set
 Them thick with silver spikes?

"Oh, I have loved the lonely wild;
 There all was fresh and free,
The birds that sang, the flowers that smiled,
 Though I was but a tree.

"When many a day had passed away,
 One morn a settler came,
And cruelly felled my brother trees,
 But left me still the same.

" Within my green protecting shade,
　　With sweet, wild water nigh,
His humble home of logs he made,
　　O'er which I towered high.

"And when with weary limbs at e'en
　　He sought his welcome bed,
A king had seldom slept, I ween,
　　With loftier roof o'erhead.

"I watched him at his cheerful toil
　　Till plenty flowed about ;
A lusty life was in the soil
　　His touch brought blooming out.

"He was a worthy man, I thought,
　　And I had heard him say
How for his country he had fought
　　On many a bloody day.

"At summer noon, oft in my shade,
　　His children by his side,
He went once more his marches o'er
　　With all a soldier's pride.

"And now the soil he trod was free,
　　Though ridged with patriots' graves.

Strange that a land so won could be
  The home, alas ! of slaves.

" The years rolled on, the cot was gone,
  A mansion took its place ;
The aged settler near it slept,
  The sod above his face.

" The wild deer came to drink no more
  By moonlight from the lake ;
The wolf had sought a wilder shore,
  The panther left the brake.

" Where the wide forest used to be,
  Now flowed the yellow wheat,
And wave on wave its saffron sea
  Broke gently at my feet.

" A monster, breathing fire and steam,
  Now often crossed the plain
Swift as the wind,—the iron dream
  Of some mechanic brain.

" Another, breathed with fiercer fire,
  Upon the lake went by ;
And later, lines of trilling wire
  Were ruled along the sky.

"Alas, I sighed, for what has been,
  And what no more shall be !
But still the tide of life rolled in,
  Resistless as the sea.

" To sudden empire, rich and great,
  'The brave young nation grew;
Star after star, each star a State,
  Shone on her banner's blue.

" A city by each ocean's side
  She seated, like a queen ;
And others by her brineless seas
  And on her prairies green.

" But now a cry of treason rose,
  And skies no more were fair ;
A gloom, a chill, a threat of ill
  Were in the uneasy air.

" Woe to that land and to that race,
  Though fortune long be kind,
Where Glory holds the foremost place
  While Justice hides behind !

As some hot cloud that, far away,
  Gathers in gloom and strength,

Thunders and threatens all the day,
　　And furious comes at length,

" So o'er a nation foul with wrong—
　　A country slavery-cursed—
The cloud of war that threatened long
　　With earthquake-fury burst.

" Oh ! speak not of that dreadful spring,
　　Name not its fears again,
For even Nature failed to bring
　　Her usual gladness then.

" The only and the anxious thought
　　Was of the rising war ;
The bloom and brightness that she brought
　　Rejoiced the world no more.

" Enough to know that they whose blood
　　Was poured like summer rain,
Whose graves are thick in field and wood,
　　Have perished not in vain.

" Thy winds, O Freedom ! blown to-day
　　From mountain-tops or waves,
Nowhere, with joy I hear them say,
　　Become the breath of slaves !

" Was it this happy end to see
  That Heaven delayed my fall?
Hail, liberal land ! where all are free,
  Are free and equal all !

"Let some resistless wind advance,
  Or 'gainst my top so high
The lightning break its fiery lance,—
  I'm ready now to die."

But still, firm-rooted in the land,
  With branches waving wide,
The old Pine towers green and grand
  Its native lake beside.

SIXTY-EIGHT AND SIXTY-NINE.

(IN THE MANNER OF PRAED.)

"There is no new thing, my friend."—CHARLES DIX.

THE sun is faithful to the sky :
  He brings the promised morrow ;
The midnight saw the Old Year die,
  And no one seems to sorrow.
The old man rises with a sigh,
  But age and ache give warning ;

The youth is glad, he knows not why,
    To meet the New Year morning.
Ah! birth is new, and death is old,
    The greater rules the lesser;
And he who lieth dumb and cold
    Hath left a brave successor.
So, let the dead Year lie in state,
    We court the next in line:
The world is done with Sixty-eight
    And ready for Sixty-nine.

There are some men to whom a sigh
    Is sweeter sound than laughter,
And some so dull that when they die
    Care not if joy live after.
They grieve that earth will warm with spring,
    While they are growing colder,
And would not have one lovely thing
    Exist if they must moulder.
But he would scorn the selfish throng,
    The Year so generous-hearted,
And would not have us mourn too long
    O'er things that have departed.
"Away! away!" would the Old Year say,
    "Night and the grave are mine."
Then leave the silent Sixty-eight
    For the living Sixty-nine.

And so we seek, in the world's wide track,
  The fields our feet are worn to,
And drop out sentiment, and go back
  To the matters we were born to.
And many will feel, and some will say,
  To self if not each other,
How dreadfully, in a general way,
  One year is like another !
What will be has already been :
  Politics to satiety,
With an earthquake or a war thrown in
  To make up a variety ;
Mosquitoes early, and house-flies late,
  With the same old sun to shine,—
We must take the old of Sixty-eight
  For the new of Sixty-nine.

Death will hurry his millions off,
  And Life produce them faster ;
And every mail will bring its tale
  Of changes and disaster.
Thieves will steal, and banks will break,
  And murders be committed ;
Small rogues be punished for justice' sake,
  And greater ones acquitted.
Of shipwrecks there will be no lack,
  Nor of floods and conflagrations,

And railway trains will leave the track,
　　With the usual aggravations.
And all that happens, and much that don't,
　　In many a startling line,
Will the press relate, as in Sixty-eight,
　　For the readers of Sixty-nine.

"Bulls" and "bears" will throng the town,
　　With looks now bright, now pallid,
And gold go up, and gold go down,
　　Like "the world" in Kingsley's ballad.
Courtships will go on, of course,
　　And Tom outrival Harry;
Last year's married seek divorce,
　　And last year's lovers marry.
The exquisite will wear his "tights,"
　　And the laborer his patches,
And Congress may take, for the latter's sake,
　　The heavy tax off matches.
The Grecian Bend perhaps will end,
　　And relieve the human spine;
But follies as great as of Sixty-eight
　　We shall see in Sixty-nine.

The papers of the growing grain
　　Trite prophecies will utter,

And buyers another year complain
  Of the shocking price of butter.
And people will love dearly still
  Their neighbors' faults to mention,
And think too much of others' sins
  To give their own attention ;
And o'er and o'er a sinner's fall
  Will tell with such a spirit,
You're forced to think that, after all,
  They're rather pleased to hear it.
Let sages frown and preachers prate,
  Alas ! we're not divine,
And the human nature of Sixty-eight
  Will flourish in Sixty-nine.

It is not things, but we, that change,—
  Not always for the better.
Perhaps the spirit's wider range
  Is free from fall and fetter.
Our earth-life is a restless chase;
  With faltering feet or steady
We hasten to that silent place
  The year has reached already.
But love will ever conquer fear,
  Joy quite forsake us never;
Some blessed hope is always near,
  Some good remains forever.

So, "with a heart for any fate,"
We join Life's marching line,
With a last good-by to Sixty-eight
And a cheer for Sixty-nine.

THE CHEERFUL SLAVE.

I.

Bound! bound!
Gold is king;
Gold is king,
And long been crowned,
Silver is an
Honored peer;
I a base
Plebeian thing,
All ungifted
With the grace
Of prince or lord;
All unworthy
To come near,
Save when lifted
From my poor
State obscure,

With no odor
Of the boor,
As the Sword
I dare appear.

II.

Toil! toil!
Day and night,
In the sea
And in the soil,
While those honored
Idlers lie,
Undefiled
And fair and bright,
Scorning as I
Pass them by,
Plodding in my
Peasant plight.
Humbly, illy
I compare
With their proud
Patrician air.

III.

Servant, slave,
Yet friend of all,

Few such service
Ever gave
As I give
In hut and hall,—
Give and ever
Give, though small
Be my pay
In thought or thank.
'Tis enough
For me to live,
Kingly only
In my uses,
In the good
My life diffuses.
So, content,
I take my rank.

PERPLEXED.

DESPITE of good and gain,
Our human doubts remain,
And even dare arraign
The Great Goodness in an unholy light.
Such doubts come over me;
I look around and see
Things that I can but question,—"Are they right?"

No voice replies from out the silences,
And further doubt my only answer is.

The world seems full of. wrong;
The weak obey the strong;
Rights, that to men belong
As sacredly as love belongs to God,
Power's ruthless bands invade,
And men once free are made
Lowly obedient to the tyrant's nod.
Thou sayest, Lord, that vengeance rests with Thee;
Then why so oft goes the oppressor free?

The rich have wealth increased;
And foremost at the feast
Sit those who gathered least
Through all the busy summer's heat and dust.
The peasant, whose sad toil
Secured the harvest spoil,
Stands humbly waiting for the broken crust;
And when the revel of his lord is o'er,
Receives his mite, nor dares to ask for more.

Has good its sure reward?
In strife 'gainst error's sword
Truth's champions have poured
Their reddest blood in vainest offering;

And Time's best age has seen
Man's fellow, poor and mean,
Scourged, bleeding, bound,—a toiling, groaning thing
Yet lands that bind and lands that break the chain
Have equal blessing of the sun and rain.

The dust of strife surrounds,
And from its gloom resounds
The noise of Life's great conflict, loud and nigh;
"God helps the weaker side!"
"Oh! then, why does He hide
The signs of its sure triumphing?" I cry.
A whisper caught from the swift winds that passed,
Made sweetest answer to my listening ear:
"Be still, sad heart; all things shall be made clear
At last, at last."

GENTLE RAIN.

AND thou hast come once more
To bless us, gentle rain!
From yonder cloudy shore
Thy light wave rolls again.

Earth's high blue roof till now
Seemed blazing all about,

Fired by the sun ! but thou
   Hast put the wide flames out.

With the fierce pomp of storm
   Thou art not rushing nigh ;
No thunders loud alarm,
   Closed is the lightning's eye.

His song th' unfrightened bird
   Still pours in yonder tree,
Whose dripping leaves are stirred
   Less by the wind than thee.

Adown the dimming sky
   The cooled delicious day
Sinks softly as a sigh,
   And still thy small drops play.

This is my dream of death,—
   After the glare and heat,
A gently failing breath,
   Calmed and content and sweet.

And some delicious sound,
   Like thine, sweet rain, to fill
My ear before the round
   Of life shall stand quite still.

Then I would close mine eyes,
    Sure that the dawn would be
Fair as to-morrow's skies
    Shall witness, after thee !

FACES AT THE WINDOW.

IN quiet village or noisy town,
    I love, as I wander through streets and lanes,
When day is up or when night is down,
    To watch the faces that come to the panes,
        By windows of houses high and grand,
        By those of the humblest in the land,—
The lordly home of the millionaire,
    And the dark abodes of shame and sin,
Seldom I pass that I do not care
'   To see what faces may be within.

Some look out so happy and round,
    Some so wan and haggard and wild ;
I wonder if ever the first have frowned,
    And if the others have ever smiled.
        Ah ! wonderful faces I often meet
        In my portrait-gallery of the street ;
Some with brows like an open book,
    Whose thoughts you can read like the printed page,

And *one*, wrinkled and old, with a look
    That I like to have belong to age.

'Tis that of a snowy-haired old man ;
    He lives in a poor and lowly place,
But I go that way whenever I can,
    Just to glance at his saintly face ;
        Lonely and gray, I know he has given
        Up every hope but that of heaven.
He has lived through many and sorrowful days,--
    I heard his story once, with a sigh ;
But I hardly pity him, for he will gaze
    Soon out of the windows of the sky.

Sometimes 'tis the face of a fond young wife
    That is looking out where the curtains part,
In her arms a little and laughing life,
    And a mother's happiness in her heart ;
        And I know she is waiting there to greet
        The coming of absent and loving feet.
How sure is the glance of her tender eye !
    She leaves the window and goes to the door ;
She has seen a form that will not pass by ;
    It bends to hers, and her watching is o'er.

Stern, rough faces, and faces fair ;
    Faces that seldom have known a tear ;

Thoughtful faces, and faces of care ;
   All by turns at the window appear.
     And often and often I hear, as I pass,
     A patter of fingers against the glass,
And a glimpse of childish brows I catch,—
   Oh, beautiful living pictures of youth !
Heaven forever over them watch,
   And keep them bright with the tints of truth !

But turn from such, and wander with me
   From the golden light and fresh, free air,
To poverty's wretchedest haunts, and see
   The faces that look from the windows there.
     Some so sunken and thin and pale,
     Telling of want a pitiful tale ;
Some whose eyes have a glare of hate ;
   And others, oh, God ! I can see them now,
Stony and dark and desolate,
   With not a sign of soul on the brow.

But the saddest of all I see are those
   I sometimes find in the darkening street,
When the rude wind of the winter blows,
   And the air is chill with frost and sleet.
     Poor little faces *outside* of the pane,
     White with the snow or wet with the rain,

Gazing wistfully in from the cold,
　　Bright with a glow that does not warm.
Poor little lambs with never a fold,
　　Poor little wanderers in the storm.

Oh, faces that look from lofty home,
　　Or from the roofs where the wretched go,
Oh, simple, quiet faces that come
　　To cottage windows, narrow and low,
　　　Oh, glad faces that make *me* glad,
　　　Oh, sad faces that make *me* sad,
Is there not coming a perfect day
　　When you all with a common love will shine,
After the worm has eaten this clay,
　　Moulded in image of Him divine?

TO-DAY.

　　Not well for him who to the past
　　　A blind faith pins;
　　Not always where one age toiled last
　　　The next begins,
　　For centuries from Time's womb cast
　　　Are not born twins.

New truth awakes to us each day,
 And its strong tide
Our poor weak hands may never stay;
 But far and wide,
It sweeps our old landmarks away
 On every side.

Away with those who set their store
 By ancient creeds;
The vain philosophies of yore
 Are not our needs;
To-day the world is calling for—
 Not words, but deeds.

JOHN GREENLEAF WHITTIER.

In one of the apartments of a private dwelling-house in Philadelphia is a marble mantel, bearing on its front a small oval mark or blur, the work of nature, which is recognized by all to whom it is pointed out as an exact picture of the poet John G. Whittier. The polish of the marble gives an exquisite finish to this unique portrait, and the following lines are suggested by the beauty and singularity of the whole.

DOTH Nature love her poet so,
 That she delights to trace
Upon the marble's spotted snow
 The soulful singer's face?

How match her love-proofs with our own,
 Be hers sweet chance or art !
She paints his features on the stone,
 And we upon the heart.

STILL YOUNG.

INSCRIBED TO R. B.

THY form is bowed with age, my friend,
 And thou hast passed thy life's full prime ;
Thou near'st the inevitable end,
 But with no terror of the time.

Thine aged face long since has lost
 The freshness of an earlier day,
And on thy head has gathered frost
 That summer suns melt not away.

And yet like those thou dost not seem
 Who in the later walks of life
Review the traveled path, and deem
 It one long way of pain and strife.

Thy blood along thy veins may start
 With slower coursing than of old,

And yet it comes not from a heart
  That years have power to render cold.

Earth still for thee with beauty glows,
  And things of joy and love are born;
Dark skies yet brighten, and the rose
  Still gives its fragrance with the thorn.

Though dimness o'er the vision creep,
  And roses from the cheek depart,
They never can be old who keep
  The joyous youth-time of the heart.

O'er thee Faith holds her wings, and, like
  A mother-bird upon the nest,
Keeps off the coldness that would strike
  The summer from thy hopeful breast.

The beauty that around us lies,—
  And when is beauty from our sight?—
Thou gratefully dost recognize,
  Not as temptation, but delight.

Some there have been—some there are still—
  So dull, so virtuous, so severe,
That it appears to them an ill
  To gather daily pleasures here.

The innocent and fine delights
  Which Heaven surely meant for all
As portion of our needs and rights,
  They can but fair temptations call.

Such narrowness thou dost condemn.
  There *is* religion e'en in art ;
Thou hast no sympathy with them
  Who free the mind but bind the heart.

Song is not sin, love is not lust,
  Beauty we need not tremble at ;
What shame to say God could not trust
  His human creatures more than that !

Between us and the open skies,
  Save melting clouds, there are no bars,—
O man ! thy earthly pathway lies
  Between the flowers and the stars !

And long ago, my friend, I know
  To thee was this conviction given :
Not joylessly should mortals go
  By such a pathway into heaven.

January, 1868.

TO ONE DEPARTED.

WE have seen thee in thy coffin,—
　Or thy beautiful, cold clay,—
Kissed thy dead lips once and often,
　Closed thy grave, and come away.

"It is finished,"—it is over,—
　All that sad and painful part;
Green the grass thy grave doth cover,
　Close the clay enfolds thy heart.

But now memory turneth to thee,
　Doing well her tender part;
And we see thee as we know thee,
　As thou wast—*and as thou art.*

For in spiritual feature
　Shines thy sweet face all the while;
If her dead *were* dead, dear Nature
　Could not thus rejoice and smile.

But in vain our earth-love's wooing,—
　In some far-off, radiant sphere
Thou art living, loving, doing,
　Now as always,—but not here!

Ah, not here! and we have only
　Tender memories of thee left;
While the crowded world seems lonely,
　Of thy presence bright bereft.

Ne'er again thy smile will greet us,
　Though its light we hunger for;
Never will thy form, to meet us,
　Glide like sunshine to the door.

Friend, adviser, sister, mother,—
　These were all in thee combined;
Fare thee well! there is no other
　Like thee for our hearts to find.

THE GRASS.

HAIL to you, my cheerful friend,
　Whom I meet with everywhere,
In whom use and beauty blend
　Perfectly as light with air.
You do not, I fear, receive
　Half the praise that is your due,
Though I never will believe
　That your friends are few.

Heel and hoof upon you trample,
   Yet, to see it if we care,
You afford a sweet example
   Of what patient faith can bear.
When the battle's bloody dew
   Dieth on the broken sod,
Quick to hide the painful hue
   From the sight of God,

Into your own guiltless growth
   You absorb the awful stain,
Planting life and beauty both
   In the red footprints of Cain !
When straightway you softly creep
   To the graves of friends and foes,
And alike above their sleep
   Spread your green repose.

Many a lesson true you teach us,
   Many a wholesome hint you give,
Many a silent sermon preach us,
   In the lowly life you live.
Though the tree above you towers,
   Envy with you is not found ;
Pride you have not, though the flowers
   Show it all around.

Very lowly is your station,
  But you pine not at your place,—
There is no humiliation
  Known to cheerfulness and grace.
Ever toiling you are seen,
  All the land you wander through,
Till you spread your grateful green
  Broad as heaven's *blue.*

In the city, which the sorest
  Needs you for its crimes and pains,
In the temples of the forest,
  Where a constant sabbath reigns,
Round our homesteads, round our graves,
  Loved by all, you wander free;
Oft the dying vision craves
  Its last glimpse of you shall be.

Voiceless and yet full of voices
  Are you, and I love to lie
With you when the year rejoices,
  'Neath the open summer sky.
Who shall say that when the heats
  Of the ripe June on you shine,
That the life that in you beats
  Is not kin to mine?

8*

Far from passion, pain, and riot,
　On the meadow's flowery floor,
Oh to feel your cooling quiet !
　Heaven's rest need be no more !
At such times, forsake me, Care !
　Busy brain, your working cease !
Earth is downy, and the air
　An expanded peace.

All the world may wander by me :
　Am I faint,—you give me rest ;
Am I lonely,—you supply me
　With companionship the best. .
Doubt our human love who can ?
　Not I ; yet I never drew
Sweeter sympathy from man
　Than I find in you.

To assert it may be sin,
　But I dare to think it true :
Nothing on the earth has been,
　Since the Christ, so good as you.
Courage, constancy, and love—
　You are active type of all.
Who more works or faith can prove ?
　Neither John nor Paul !

HARVEST-TIME.

I.

SLOWLY the starlight fades away ;
A faintest tinge of reddening gray
Flames in the East's low horizon, heraldic of the coming
day.

II.

The pale moon hides her silver horn,
And, on the rising breezes borne,
A hundred waking voices break the dewy silence of the
morn.

III.

From tangled brake and leafy hill
Goes up the birds' rejoicing trill,
Till all the listening skies above with Nature's sweet-
tuned music fill.

IV.

And as the songsters gayly chime,
The first young beams of morning climb
And mingle in one glare, to light the long, glad hours
of harvest-time.

V.

Bright o'er the earth the full day breaks;
The sleeping world to life awakes,
And rested Labor leaves his couch and to his toil
    himself betakes.

VI.

Forth to the field, a sturdy throng,
The harvesters, with laugh and song,
From many a farm-house white outpour and haste
    .with earnest step along.

VII.

Slow moving through the ripened fields,
His gleaming blade the reaper wields
With tireless arm; and, falling low, the waiting
    grain unto him yields.

VIII.

And, following close, the binder leaves
His pathway strewn with yellow sheaves,
That rustle in the summer wind like rain-drops on
    dead autumn leaves.

IX.

Upon the harvest air there steals
The roll of verdure-muffled wheels,
As onward pass the patient teams, the wain low
    rumbling at their heels.

X.

Halted among the gathered sheaves,
    A precious freight it quick receives,
Then, winding o'er the stubble slopes, unloads beneath
    the sheltering eaves.

XI.

As thus they reap the fruitful lands,
    Oh! let us humbly clasp our hands,
And in all truth and reverence ask God's blessing on
    the harvest bands!

SUMMER HYMN.

A VISIBLE blessing rests upon the land,
    With joy the heart of man was never sweeter;
Summer has almost reached the Autumn's hand,
    That seems outstretched to greet her.
Her work is done, and to her rest she goeth,
    Making a fragrance of her dying breath,
While round her path a golden glory gloweth,
    Lighting her steps to death.

It is a solemn hour, and yet not sad;
    The corn-fields rustle, and the waters glisten,

The forests sweep around us green and glad,
   With music in each leaflet if we listen.
And they know, and, knowing, are subdued,
   In all their joy, that Summer's strength is failing;
There is a tenderness in Nature's mood
   That soon will wake to wailing.

A lovelier season never on us smiled,
   Her presence seemed so living and so human;
Spring was the wayward and capricious child,
   Summer the loving woman.
We part from her as from a cherished friend
   Who unto gentle, painless death is given,
And on whose face remaineth to the end
   A look as if of heaven.

Unblamed, may we not think there is a spirit
   Of the departed Summer that survives,
And in some higher region doth inherit
   The crown of perfect lives?
If this should be, what glory must await
   The beauteous season, not yet quite departed!
Faithful was she in her first estate,
   Full-handed and free-hearted.

Never had toil more liberal reward,
   More bountiful was not Earth's first fruition;

Her ancient vigor seems almost restored,
   And hope is man's condition.
God of the harvest! all good gifts Thou hast given :
   Sunlight and dew, and most the blessed rain,
That, 'twixt the green of earth, the blue of heaven,
   Swung glad its silver chain.

We thank Thee that once more our eyes behold
   The miracle of Nature's resurrection ;
While not a grass-blade grew, nor blossom swelled,
   Outside of Thy protection.
The snow's delay, the sunshine's recompense,
   The mountain's and the meadow's gradual green-
      ing,—
On all we looked, with no diminished sense
   Of their sublimer meaning.

Disastrous blight, as sometimes, came not near,
   Nor War and Pestilence, those dread marauders;
Untimely frosts did not descend to sear ;
   No fierce tornado crossed our fruitful borders.
In peace we watched the days come up in splendor ;
   The dreamy noons soft-sunk in sunny rest ;
The many-colored sunsets burning tender,
   Like mornings in the west.

How full of God seemed all those glowing hours !
   Nature rebuked the skeptic and the doubter;

Faith took again the simple form of flowers,
  While Love rejoiced about her.
That time is past, and now the shortening days
  Hint of decay and take a tinge of sadness,
But still are full of pleasantness and praise,—
  The after-harvest gladness.

Soon fiercely forth invading winds will rush
  Through mountain pass and under forest column,
And northern nights come down with frigid hush,
  Unpitying and solemn.
Welcome that time of tempest and of snow!
  The skies will still repeat their starry story,
And through the gloom a future Summer show,
  Crowned with the olden glory.

  August 28, 1869.

TOHICKON.

Sweet, quiet spot! it was a summer noon
  When first amid thy solitudes I strayed;
As if thyself had bid, with joyous tune,
  Thy songsters welcome to thy rest and shade.

Bright shone the sun in rich meridian glare,
  And all thy trees waved invitation sweet,

As the warm pulses of the dreamy air
  Softly among their screening branches beat.

We were a merry band,—for not alone
  I sought to pass those few swift hours with thee ;
Thy beauteous haunts, I ween, had seldom known
  The presence of a goodlier company.

Where the thick curtains of thy woods, o'erhead
  Drawn green and dim, cast down their coolest shade,
Around a rock, that maidens' hands had spread
  With plenteous feast, a full repast we made.

Then down thy slopes, that green before us lay,
  Into thy low, delightful vale we strolled ;
By rugged path and tangled winding way
  We flanked thy heights, precipitous and bold.

Thy loneliest nook had felt the thirsty gleam
  Of the ripe sunshine falling hot and red,
And, from its banks, we saw thy famished stream
  With rippled surface creep along its bed.

Here, dark and still, it wound its current where
  The cooling shadows of thy cliffs were thrown,
And farther on, 'gainst bars that, brown and bare,
  Were interposed, it broke with lowly moan.

As by its sides I watched the white groups pass,
  Or saw them o'er it bend with perfect grace,
It seemed to smile, I thought, when, like a glass,
  It gave reflection of some lovely face.

Then on again with sluggish, devious flow,
  It purled and fretted by thy rocky piles;
Its waters scant with bubbles all aglow,
  That wrecked themselves against its little isles.

The autumn rains would fall, I knew, until,
  With generous floods its every source supplied,
The sleeping echoes of thy russet hill
  Would wake in answer to its roaring tide.

*   *   *   *   *   *   *

The hours sped on; the sun, low in the skies,
  Warned that we could no longer with thee dwell;
So from thy scenes we turned our lingering eyes,
  When to them we had looked a long farewell.

Yet to thee oft, Tohickon, I will turn,
  When memory leads me in her gentle train;
Thy charms I will recall, until I yearn
  To feel their holy influence again.

When, by the troubled days in which we live,—
  Their rude alarms, their strifes that never cease,—

I am oppressed, if then to thee I give
  One moment's thought, that moment will be peace.

Sweet hermit spot ! with thee the home might be
  Of those who from their fellows live alway,—
Stern anchorites, and sages gray,—ah me !
  The world would only laugh at such to-day !

And yet in haunts like thine, far from the sound
  Of noisy reasoning and vain dispute,
Men truly wise and good there might be found,
  As thickest foliage hides the rarest fruit.

Thine is no classic ground ; but, lone and fair,
  A garden-place, by Nature planned, thou art ;
Where the wild Beautiful may be, and where
  The fading works of man can have no part.

Were I to come, when I had passed my youth,
  Once more amid thy loveliness to range,
The same old scenes would speak the sad, sad truth :
  It is not *things*, so much as *men*, that change.

August, 1864.

A DAY IN OCTOBER.

I WANDER far by field and glen,
　The hazy skies are hanging low ;
The breeze awhile is strong, and then
　　　　Forgets to blow.
His curious web the spider weaves
　O'er late-green acres growing brown ;
Like wounded birds, the colored leaves
　　　　Are fluttering down.
As red are those yon maple shows
　As if the drops that wet the wood
　Last night had not been rain, but blood.

Of berries bright the hedge is full ;
　The bay-bush blushes as with shame ;
The sumach's plume is like a dull
　　　　But steady flame.
Erect the pointed poplars stand,
　Proud to display their fluttering gold ;
The rough pine towers green and grand,
　　　　Unhurt by cold.
The scarlet brier seems all on fire,

And in the breeze the golden-rod
Waves stiffly o'er the frosted sod.

At times the bright woodpecker knocks
    With sound that seems the wood to jar;
The wild fowl northward fly in flocks
                Triangular.
Beyond the upland, sear and dry,
    On which the scattered heaps of corn
Like spots of yellower sunshine lie,
                A smoke is borne
In languid drifts; then white uplifts,
    And, like some earth-freed spirit fair,
    Ascends the steep and stairless air.

I leave the upland, broad and bright,
    And to the hoary woodland stray;
There, with a solemn, softened light,
                Shines the still day.
Oh, beautiful! through stained glass
    Never such light as this did pour;
Almost in awe along I pass;
                A marble floor,
Instead of moss, I seem to cross,
    As if my feet, invading, trod
    Some inmost sanctuary of God.

9*

INDIAN SUMMER.

THE Autumn, brown and late, is forth,
    Yet storms delay awhile ;
A sweet, sad light is over earth,—
    'Tis Summer's dying smile.
From field and fern she could not go,
    And all she loved before,
Without one last fond look, and so
    She comes to them once more.

As we go last to look on some
    Dear face whence life has fled,
So doth the mourner Summer come
    To gaze upon her dead.
The Autumn marks her features wan,
    And, seeing that she grieves,
He comforts her as best he can,
    And strews her paths with leaves.

The chilling winds he doth repress
    Which would about her blow,
And shows by his rough tenderness
    That he respects her woe.

Ah ! little he can for her do;
　　He brings no rainbow-showers;
He cannot tint her hills anew,
　　Nor give her back her flowers.

And when her pensive eyes behold
　　The change wrought by decay,
She feels her feeble limbs grow cold,
　　Her heart-warmth pass away.
And, with that sad smile on her face,
　　She lowly droops her head
In tender and expiring grace,
　　And dies beside her dead.

THE FROST.

I COME, I come from my Arctic halls,
Where the iceberg rears its glittering walls,
And the billows break with a sullen roar
'Gainst the snowy cliffs of the polar shore.

I have lingered long in a cheerless clime,
While the year has had its bud and prime,
And the golden harvest sprung from the sod
Of the desert fields that the winter trod.

As one for a triumph waits, so I·
Have lain, while the sun in the southern sky
Sank lower down, and shortened his march
Through the glowing space of the azure arch.

For not till his sultry strength was spent,
And his fire-shod feet retreating went
Toward the South's bright gates, dared I venture forth
From my fortress home in the frozen North.

Over mountain and plain, away, away!
I follow the track of the flying day;
And the green earth thrills with a silent fear,
As she feels me come with the darkness near.

With crystal bridges I span the streams,
And onward I sweep 'neath the moon's cold beams,
Till not a lone spot is there left uncrossed
By the flying form of the demon Frost.

Where I scatter the flakes of my driftless snow,
The light of the rosy morn will show
The beautiful wonders my hand has wrought,
Swift as the whirlwind, silent as thought.

To the dim, hushed woods in my flight I turn,
And to-morrow their fated leaves will burn

With a hundred hues, as false as the glow
That flushes the cheek when the life is low.

The chestnuts drop at the touch of my wand,
And the shellbarks, brushed by my viewless hand,
Rebound from the turf or plash in the rill,
Though the loaded boughs of the trees are still.

Oh, joy for the groups that at early morn
Come brushing their way through the wet-leafed corn,
When they find, 'neath the colored leaves they stir,
The scattered wealth of the hull and burr!

The grass, the corn, and the late green wheat
Feel the icy tread of my silent feet,
And soon to take they will all be seen
The Autumn's brown for the Summer's green.

Alas for the flowers! to them my breath
Is like a blast from a land of death;
Though some bloom on as if they knew
That the blighting frost is but colder dew.

But though I bring to the fields so gay
A terror that takes their gladness away,
Though the bloom and fragrance of sun-grown things
Must fade when I pass on my shadowy wings.

Yet a sweeter air and a lovelier sky
Shall follow me far as I hasten by;
And though clouds succeed, and white storms fall,
A promise of life lies warm in them all.

Beyond the darkness, beyond the cold,
The map of the Spring is in beauty unrolled;
And glory and brightness descend to the Earth,
As they did when the stars rejoiced at her birth!

As frost to the fields, so death comes to men;
They perish—but only to flourish again.
So, mortals, take courage, and fear not the blast
That blows when the summer of life is past.

THE ICE-KING. -

In the far regions of the North there dwells a monarch
    grim,
King of those ever-frozen realms, that, unexplored and
    dim,
Are spread around the distant pole, and, dumb and
    dead and white,
Lie always in the shadow of one grand, eternal night.

A mighty king is he ;
No other king may be,
Of all earth's sovereign rulers, so much a king as he.

We feel the bitter north wind blow,—it only is his
    breath ;
Like arctic darkness is his frown, his very look is death ;
And never to his presence dread dare mortal's footsteps
    go,—
He is a hermit and a king, and in his robes of snow,
        Grand, terrible, and lone,
        He sits upon his throne,
The never-dying monarch of an ever-freezing zone.

Loyal his subjects are, but few,—the frost, the cloud,
    the storm,
Obedient to his least behest, around his awful form
Gather their might, or speed away o'er his dominions
    far ;
Free even as himself, yet they his willing servants are :
        No trembling vassal stands
        To list to his commands,
For he no king of people is, but of unpeopled lands.

Built of the glittering, silver ice, his palaces arise,
Their shining turrets reaching towards the cold stars in
    the skies.

Cities of purest ice he rears, and paves with ice the
    streets,
Breaks off the icebergs from his shores, and sails them
    as his fleets,
          And o'er his drear domain,
          Upon each hill and plain,
He hoards the deep, abundant snows, and counts them
    as his gain.

When he is weary with the shade of his long lowering
    nights,
Within the hollow skies he sets his wild, mysterious
    lights,
That, flaming through the viewless air, in our own
    heavens shine,
And of his kingdom's glories are a beauteous, wondrous
    sign,—
          Strange meteors 'mid the gloom,
          His borders they illume,
And are his frigid fires that burn and yet do not con-
    sume.

Across the torrid main he floats his crystal argosies,
And white upon the mountain-tops he plants his colo-
    nies ; ·

Sends his stern ministers each year to desolate the
    earth,
And binds her flowery, Eden fields within an icy girth,—
        A cruel king he is ;
He spoils the realms of other kings, but they cannot
    spoil his.

We love our green and sunny slopes, he loves his polar
    home ;
Beneath the forest's leafy arch our feet may gayly
    roam ;
Our eyes may watch the warm waves toss and the bright
    rivers flow;
He lives apart from our delights, a hermit-king,—and
    though
        No flowers for him unfold,
        No harvests lift their gold,
Yet joyously he reigns amid his solitudes of cold.

THE WINTER NIGHT AND THE SUMMER NOON.

THE moon is down, and the night is chill,
　The silent snow-flakes flutter and fall,
And the stars, that I know are in the skies,
　Through the gloom I cannot see at all.

Here, where the firelight falls so clear,
　Flooding the room with a rosy tide,
I sit, as the sombre hours wear on,
　And list to the moan of the storm outside.

Its warning given, twelve measured strokes
　The old clock peals from the chimney-shelf,
In tones as solemn and weird and strange
　As if 'twere the voice of time itself.

Bleaker without grows the lonely night,
　And, as louder the troubled blast complains,
Against my window I hear a sound
　As if ghostly fingers touched the panes.

'Tis only the beat of the driving flakes,
　Wilder whirled to the earth below,

Till village and vale and hill are lost
In a wide, white waste of midnight snow.

I gaze without on the desolate scene,
While a gentle sorrow comes to my breast
As I think of the beautiful year I loved
Under these snow-flakes laid at rest.

The beautiful year, with its days of light,
Its cheeks of rose, and its garlanded brow,
Its brooks, its birds, and its forests green,
Its flowers and harvests,—where are they now?

The streams are hushed, and the birds are flown,
And the flowers, since the frost put out their bloom,
Under their shroud of snow have lain,
Like friends of ours in the silent tomb.

But why should I sigh? for the spring will come,
And break for the streams their icy chain;
The earth will awake from its sleep of death,
And blossom and bloom with beauty again.

And, if for the dead of the woods and fields
This beautiful future shall come to pass,
Oh! what of the dead that we have lost?
Can they be less than the leaves and grass?

Blow, blow, ye winds from the stormy north,
　And drift, ye snows from the sullen skies !
Still through the wail of the storm I hear
　Faith on her rustling pinions rise.

And I will not set my songs of life
　To slow and sorrowful tunes,
For there isn't a year with its winter nights
　But there follow the summer noons.

What though the tempest roar o'erhead,
　And the land be drear as the frozen pole ?
There's a summer noon of light for the earth,
　A summer noon of life for the soul !

THE STREAM OF THE VALLEY.

Thou murmuring stream !
Whose silver length shines through the purple valley,
Beside thy banks oft have I loved to dally,
And feel the peace that thou art ever bringing ;
　And see thy smiles, and hear thy song,
　As windingly thou flowest along,
With ripples for thy smiles, and rippling for thy singing.

Since God's great hand
Unbarred for thee the green gates of the mountains,
And led thee, laughing, from thy secret fountains
Down to the margin of the far-off river,
    The years have seen thee glide,
    With dimpled, bubbled tide,
Ever changing in thy flow, and yet unchanged forever.

On morns of spring,
Oft have I watched the early sunshine flashing,
First on the hills, and then along the meadow,
Scaring before it every lingering shadow,
    Waking the wild flags from their dewy dreams,
    And gliding on until at last it seems
To stoop and drink where thy bright waves are dashing.

When summer skies,
Unclouded, overarch thee, hot and glowing,
    And all thy flowers drop their modest eyes,
    Afraid to look upon their lord, the sun,
    Close to their feet they hear thy waters run,
And turn to thee, and watch thee in thy flowing;
    And then I fancy that their dumb lips move,
    As if to thank thee for thy care and love,
Until, at times, the impulse half obeying,
    I bend my ear, that I may hear
What words of blessing they to thee are saying.

But when the autumn brings
The Indian-summer hours of pale October,
    And all dull things
Are glad, and all glad things are sober,
    Most to thy presence do my footsteps stray;
The crimson leaves that are thy bosom staining
    Float on thy surface, like dead hopes, away,—
They and thy waters going, but thou fore'er remaining.

    But whether morning's light
Plays by thy brink, or whether golden-hearted
Summer skies in glory burn above thee,
    Or whether autumn gales
    Breathe out their mournful tales
Of a sweet summer that has just departed,
Thou art the same, and 'tis for this I love thee.

THE LAND OF NEVERMORE.

THERE is a land forever
    Unchanged by change, though never,
Save in memory and dreams, our feet can tread its shore;
    It is that pleasant region
    Where dwell the shining legion
Of things that have departed,—the land of Nevermore.

And unto its dominions,
Conveyed upon the pinions
Of tender recollection, who does not love to go ?
For all that has been sweetest,
Or fairest, or completest,
In the lives that we have lived, we there again may
know.

To some it may be lonely,—
To those who have had only
A few faint joys to brighten the pathway of their
years;
Yet even these the daytime
Of youth—life's sunny Maytime—
Have known and have enjoyed, and there it reappears.

Ay, there the old and weary,
Approaching fast death's dreary
And terror-haunted valley, resume awhile their youth;
And bosoms filled with sadness
May thrill once more with gladness,
And lips of the deceiver may find again their truth.

And there the mother presses
Her babe with soft caresses,—
That clear-eyed babe whose laughter so long ago was
husbed ;

The maiden her lost lover
Finds in their trysting-cover,
Where first the sweet confession to hear and make she
blushed.

Love-words, so gently spoken,
And promises now broken—
Forgetting that they are so—we there may hear again;
Or grasp some former treasure,
Or feel anew some pleasure
From which time has extracted the poison-sting of pain.

And restless-souled Ambition,
That from its poor condition
Once thought to have arisen high in fame's noontide
beam,
Now, hopeless and defeated,
And still as lowly seated,
Back to that land may wander, and dream again its
dream.

Warm hearts may now be near us,
Bright eyes may shine to cheer us,
And forms of loved and loving within our homes may
stand;
But warmer hearts and truer,
And brighter eyes and bluer,
And faces still more lovely, are in that other land.

No Present is there o'er it,
No Future stands before it,
Uncertain and portentous, and full of fear and doubt;
Nor blight nor storm can enter,
To make our spring a winter
And change our day to darkness, if we choose to keep
them out.

Then, years, so swiftly gliding,
So short with us abiding,
That you go by so quickly no longer we deplore;
For we would greatly rather
That you would pass, and gather
Into these fadeless ages—the years of Nevermore!

THE MYSTERY.

OH ! what a strange being this creature is
That hath the earth so under his sway !
For all things below him seem wholly his,
To rule and use them as he may,—
To come and go whenever he bids,
Nor question nor dispute his way.

He wandereth up, and he wandereth down,
In a sort of strange unrest,

As though he oft sought, but never found,
   A quiet for his breast;
A pillow of perfect peace his head
   I'm sure hath never pressed.

I see him abroad all over the land,
   I see him upon the main;
If I miss him a moment, I look once more,
   And then I see him again.

He buildeth a city, then teareth it down,
   Then raiseth it up once more;
And he still toils on, till his temples stand
   Where they never have stood before;
And I'm told that as he worketh now
   He hath ever worked of yore.

He taketh the hand of his fellow in love,
   And walketh in peace by his side,
Till he heareth a word, incautiously said,
   That woundeth his honor or pride,
When he turneth and rendeth his comrade in wrath,
   Or pusheth him rudely aside.

His deeds are of Greatness, of Right, and of Wrong,—
   All mingled in sorest dismay;

What seemeth at morning as noble and good
    Is evil at close of the day ;
He gives one a serpent, another a fish,
    Then carelessly goes on his way.

He holdeth outstretched, in the same open palm,
    The olive branch and the sword ;
And the empires he foundeth may flourish or fall
    On the turning of a word ;
He buildeth a palace, to die in a cot,
    And sleepeth a peasant, to wake up a lord.

At the harvest of Peace and the harvest of War
    His sickle is equally keen,
And I never have yet been able to tell
    Which field he most loveth to glean ;
For he buildeth a sheaf or taketh a life
    With the same unchanging mien.

To *me* the pages of human life
    Have never seemed open and fair,
And this much only have I learned
    In all I have studied there :
'Twas God's intention that man should be
    For Earth a master, for Heaven an heir.

July 5, 1863.

IS THE WORLD OLD OR YOUNG?

I.

Is the World old or young,—
　　A child or a man?
Who shall say when the life
　　Of the giant began?
How many years still
　　To the shine of the sun
Shall he lift his broad brow,—
　　Ten thousand or one?

II.

Speak, voices of truth,
　　Through the din of our days,
Till we know how to shape
　　Our censure or praise;
For the World, that we say
　　Groweth hoary with years,
Perhaps is not done
　　With his infantile fears.

III.

Of the knowledge, the wisdom
　　He boasts of to-day,

Like a vain, learned man,
    When his head shall be gray
May to him appear
    As the learning of youth,
To one aged grown
    In the study of truth.

IV.

The strife of his armies,
    The roll of his drums,
May be but mock battle
    To warfare that comes ;
Or a spirit so holy
    His breast may draw near,
Till the peace of the past
    Shall like turmoil appear.

V.

O men and O brethren !
    If there's one thing sublime
This side of the skies,
    It is time, it is time !
It is time,—and the World
    May be yet in his youth,
With ages on ages
    To live for the truth !

11

AT THE METROPOLIS.

ALONG the crowded street
I hear the ceaseless beat
Of myriad footsteps as they come and go ;
And gaze, as in a dream,
Upon life's busy stream,
That by me has its flow and counter-flow.

Darkly the night is down
Upon the bustling town ;
Still sweeps the human tide resistless on ;
And, with a sullen roar,
Like some rough, ocean shore,
Is ever going, and yet ne'er is gone.

Hiding the evening skies,
Grandly around me rise
The mighty city's walls, that bind the sight
To the illumined pave,
O'er which the shadows wave,
Afraid to settle on a scene so bright.

Proud City of our Land !
Within thy bounds I stand,
Where once, when thou wert not, the red men stood
    And heard the wild birds soar,
    And watched thy river pour
Into the sailless sea its unnamed flood ;

    Or, wearied with the chase,
    Lay, in their savage grace,
Beside the fires that lit their lonely camps, .
    While, dense and dark, around,
    A solemn forest frowned
Where now the air is glowing with thy lamps.

    When restless Progress spurned
    His old restraints, and turned
From the far Eastern world his vessel's prow,
    His new home here he chose,
    And, swift and fair, uprose
Beneath his hand these piles that gird me now.

    And now the once lone isle
    Doth with thy presence smile ;
Freedom's long years have heard thy steeples chime ;
    Wealth decks thee with its pride,
    And from thy harbor ride
Thy freighted ships to visit every clime.

But not for this alone,
Fair city, art thou known :
A classic river winds thee in its arms ;
Beauty within thee glows ;
Romance around thee throws
Its loveliness, and history its charms.

It glads the patriot's heart
To be with thee ; thou art
A palace beautiful and vast,—a dome
Beneath whose thousand spires
Ambition builds his fires,
And Art and Commerce have their fostering home.

NEW YORK, February 22, 1865.

ONWARD!

AY ! *this* is the watchword !
This is the cry !
Onward ! right onward,
To do or to die.

Timid and listless
Sit not and sigh,

While others, more earnest,
   Are passing you by.

Up with the foremost !
   Join in the race,
With the smile of endeavor
   Lighting your face.

Onward ! press onward !
   The *will* makes the *way ;*
Life was not meant
   As a pastime or play.

Join in the struggle,
   With zeal and with strength ;
As *others* have conquered,
   So *you* may at length.

Onward ! right onward !
   Be one of the few
Who have *courage* to dare,
   And *patience* to do.

Onward ! press onward !
   For triumph is sweet,
And the rust of inaction
   Is worse than defeat.

11*

THE WAVE.

(IN IMITATION OF SHELLEY'S "CLOUD.")

OF the dust he treads man came to be,
  And he calls his mother Earth ;
But I am born of the wind and sea,
  With the moon to watch my birth.
He may have his home where I cannot come,
  But the whole wide main is mine ;
I toss and roll by the southern pole,
  And back to the burning line.
Like a giant band, the icebergs stand
  To guard the Arctic's portals,
But I glide by their feet, and flow, till I beat
  On a shore never trod by mortals.
I cool my brow in the polar snow,
  And backward then I shiver,
Kissing the mouth, as I wander south,
  Of many a crystal river.

On the quiet bay I love to play
  When the tired wind gently lingers,
And its tangled mass of wild sea-grass
  I comb with my salty fingers.

Sunny highlands, and tropic islands,
   Wearing their crowns of palms,
I sparkle by, till I almost die
   In the regions of the calms.
Those fervid skies, with their burning eyes,
   I moan and languish under,
Till I hear afar a noise like war,—
   Its terror and its thunder.
Then the wild gull shrieks, and her nest she seeks,
   The frightened air grows hotter,
And the hurricane in his might again
   Comes rushing over the water.
When, the fiery lightning his forehead bright'ning,
   And his cloudy banners o'er him,
In his terrible wrath he sweeps on his path,
   Driving the sea before him,
In his arms so strong he bears me along,
   But I break from his rude embrace,
And rise like a wall, and totter and fall,
   And fling my foam in his face.

Oft over my sight streams a signal light,
   And I hear, with the joy of a demon,
The solemn boom roll deep through the gloom,
   From the gun of the perishing seaman.
I leap on the deck of the drifting wreck,
   And drag him into the water,—

What do I care for his mother's prayer,
   Or the tears of his wife and daughter?
His bones shall whiten where diamonds brighten
   The lower ocean's floor,
And the voice of the surge shall be his dirge,
   Sounding for evermore.

Through secret straits, to the coral gates
   Of the mermaids' palace I roam,
And gather bright shells from the ocean dells,
   To deck their watery home.
I mould the sands with my white wet hands,
   And the rough coast dent with scars;
I take my hue from the upper blue,
   And double the number of stars.
When that lady of grace—the moon—her sweet face
   . Would behold, she gazes on me;
And the sun every day, when the clouds are away,
   On my bosom his image can see.
I am the child of the breezes wild,—
   The waves of the air,—and brother am I
To the shining crowds of flying clouds
   That I call the waves of the sky!

LIFE THROUGH DEATH.

O Death, we fear thee !   All our joys and pleasures
   We feel and hold as thou alone may say :
In vain, with jealous care, we watch our treasures,
   Thou dost despoil us of them day by day.
We have our homes, and lovely things around them
   Spring up to gladden and adorn the earth ;
They bloom not long: too oft, when thou hast found
      them,
   They fade within the hour that saw their birth:
And when our sun of hope is brightest shining,
   'Tis thy strange joy to shade its beams with night,
Till gloom surrounds, and e'en the silver lining
   Upon the cloud shows pale unto our sight.
Affection's golden links are by thee riven,
   That bind us to our good, our fair, our brave,
As one by one, to thy cold keeping given,
   We bear our loved to the insatiate grave.

Thou comest nigh, and dear, familiar faces,
   Whose smiles could brighten saddest hours, we miss ;
We look around, and see the empty places,
   And know 'twas thou who stole from us our bliss.

When thou dost take what most we would retain,
    And dost our cup with sorrow over-fill,
Our robbed and wounded hearts may sore complain,
    But thou remainest unrelenting still.
We fear thee, Death! but with our fear is mingled
    Something of joy thy terrors cannot quell;
Though thou for victims hast our fairest singled,
    And cast thy darts at what we loved so well.
How far were God, what fearful space between
    This low, dim spot and Heaven's higher land,
Had not the soul, with faith's clear vision, seen
    The wide abyss by thy dark bridges spanned!

O'er thy fell work cease, then, thy ghastly grinning,
    Boast not too much of all thy awful powers;
Though cruel and strong, the triumphs thou art winning
    Are not all thine,—*thy* victories are *ours*.
For thou dost guide each weary, fainting mortal,
    When thou hast conquered, from the realms of sin;
'Tis thy dread hand unbars the heavenly portal
    And leads us to undying life within.

LINES ON A SKULL.

WRITTEN AT THE ACADEMY OF NATURAL SCIENCES, PHILADELPHIA.

BEHOLD ranged yonder, row on row,
Along the shelves in horrid show,
Those skulls, which, though no eye is there,
Seem grimly in our own to stare;
Which, though they long death's prey have been,
Have yet enough of life to grin.
By breath and warmth and soul forsook,
They make us shudder as we look.
Yet one, it seems to me, has less
Of all the common hideousness.
Something more human I can trace
Within its white and fleshless face,
Which death could not, nor yet the worm,
To utter ugliness transform.
Though now 'tis but a naked skull,
It must have been, once, beautiful.

And if some power could restore
The living eyes that once it bore,

What soulful light might from them start !
And if the lips were there to part,
The cheeks to dimple, and the chin
To catch and hold the dimples in,
How bright a smile then might we see
That fixed and ghastly grin could be !
The massive and high-builded brow
Is almost noble, even now,
And once, clear-flamed and strong, behind,
There may have glowed the fires of mind.
And these may oft the tongue have warmed
Till with its eloquence it charmed,
Or till, in some great hour, it stirred
To utter the convincing word,
With whose apt aid, perhaps, was broke
Some tyrant Error's galling yoke.

It may have been ; though why at last,
When earthly things for it were past,
This head could not be left to rot
In darkness in some chosen spot,
Where no wide eye could on it stare,
I do not know, I do not care.
I only know the deathless mind
That fled and left this ruin behind,
Somewhere within the heavenly zone
Will find and fill another throne ;

That He who lit its holy fire
Will never let the flame expire;
That when our central shining sun
His course of glory shall have run,
And stars and planets cease to turn,
Somewhere, still bright, that fire shall burn.

THE BLUE COAT AND THE GRAY.

A BALLAD OF THE REBELLION.

NEAR fair Virginia's borders
  Two youthful brothers dwelt
When treason's sad disorders
  First in the land were felt.
Sons were they of a mother
  Who loved them passing well,
But brother's heart 'gainst brother
  With hate began to swell.
For one forgot his country,
  And one to her proved true;
One put on the gray coat,
  And one put on the blue.

The mother blessed the bearer
  Of the loyal Union hue,

But saw the dreadful error
   That on the other grew.
By ardent words and tender
   To win him back she strove;
He would not make surrender
   Of his ill-chosen love.
In vain her tears and pleadings;
   She saw them march away;
One he wore the blue coat,
   And one he wore the gray.

God pity her, poor woman!
   As in her woe she stands.
If 'gainst a common foeman
   They had but joined their hands,
No living loyal mother
   Had prouder been to see;
But brother against brother!
   It was too sad to be.
Led by different captains,
   They marched to join the fray;
One he wore the blue coat,
   And one he wore the gray.

The crimson wave of battle
   Rolled to her very door;

She heard the rifle's rattle,
　　The cannon's awful roar.
Her sick heart in her bosom,
　　It beat above the guns :
" My boys ! and must I lose them ?
　　My brave and darling sons !
My heart can know but sorrow
　　Whichever wins to-day,
For one is with the blue coats,
　　And one is with the gray."

At last had ceased the thunder
　　That all day long had pealed.
The sad-faced moon in wonder
　　Looked down upon the field.
What need to tell the horror
　　Those soft, sad beams lit up ?
That anguished mother ! for her
　　Remained a bitterer cup.
Two lifeless forms were borne her
　　Before the break of day ;
One had on the blue coat,
　　And one had on the gray.

She saw them, and she knew them.
　　" My God," she cried in woe,

"The blade and ball that slew them
   Oh, let me never know!"
Then equally for them caring,
   She laid them in the grave:
Although the one was erring,
   She knew they both were brave.
"All bitter memories from me,"
   She said, "I put away;
I always loved the blue coat,
   But I cannot hate the gray."

A spirit like that mother's
   Shall in *our* bosoms dwell;
No longer foes, but brothers,
   Are they who fought us well.
With the grim cannon's rattle
   Let strife and hatred cease;
The bravest in the battle
   Are manliest in peace.
Let every bitter memory
   With the war-cloud fade away;
Although we love the blue coat,
   We will not hate the gray.

THE PROMISE.

'Twas December; cold and pallid lay the dead year in
    its shroud,
Winter snows were fast descending, winter winds were
    wailing loud,
Winter seas their icy billows tossed beneath a sky of
    cloud.
Out amid the stormy darkness, on the waters wild and
    wide,
See, a gallant bark is struggling with the angry arctic
    tide !
Now she mounts the noisy surges like a thing of life
    and pride,
Now she sinks into the shadow of the ocean's briny
    wall ;
Blinded, battling, still she presses onward through the
    tempest's pall,
While the heaving floods around her, in their fury, rise
    and fall.
Oh ! the hero-crew that mans her ! Oh ! the hero-
    freight she bears !
Oh ! the hearts that beat within her, and the noble
    purpose theirs !

Oh! the spirit that, undoubting, death and danger
　　　fearless dares!

Heaven speeds that gallant vessel, sailing from Oppres-
　　　sion's realm;

Heaven helps her, vainly round her leap the waves to
　　　overwhelm;

Vainly howl the winds above her: God's own hand is
　　　at her helm.

'Tis the old heroic story, need we tell it o'er again?

Lives the Pilgrim Fathers' glory but in records of the
　　　pen?

How they left the land that bore them, where men were
　　　no longer men?

How, where proud Atlantic's waters 'gainst her western
　　　bounds are hurled,

They their tyrant-hated banner to the wilderness un-
　　　furled

O'er the holy, haunted birth-spot of a new hope for the
　　　world?

Hoary rock! that first was trodden by the free feet of
　　　our sires!

On thy summit, through the ages, glows the light of
　　　Freedom's fires,

At thy base our patriot martyrs strike their silver-
　　　sounding lyres;

Round thee, shades of heroes fallen their protecting
　　　vigils hold,

While above thee flames a *Promise*, and in shining
    words of gold,
One by one, the mighty meanings of its prophecies
    unfold ;
And the trembling nations, reading, gazing in each
    other's eyes,
Doubting, fearing, half believing, stand with looks of
    wild surprise,
As the brightness of that promise blazes in the Western
    skies.

'Tis a promise of a Future, O America, for thee,
Of a Future far outshining all thy Past has dared to be,
When shall triumph yet supremer Order, Truth, and
    Liberty.
Thee, my country, in His goodness has the God of
    nations blessed ;
Thou hast been a land of refuge for the exiled and
    oppressed,
Thou hast clothed the cold and naked, and the weary
    given rest.
Grandly have the years passed for thee since thou hadst
    thy stormy birth,
Sunny skies have smiled above thee, Plenty poured her
    fullness forth,
Foes have feared and friends have loved thee for thy
    might and for thy worth.

But a prouder day awaits thee,—Plymouth's glad apoc-
    alypse
Unturned pages of thy story with a purer radiance
    tips,
And thy deeds in coming ages shall thy olden fame
    eclipse.   .
Even now the Old World trembles at the mention of
    thy name,
While her sad, down-trodden millions, 'mid their
    wretchedness and shame,
Looking towards thee, feel their bosoms glow with
    Freedom's holy flame.
And that flame shall glow yet stronger, till their bonds
    are rent apart,
Till the peasant claims his manhood, and his quickened
    pulses start
With the fierce, ecstatic throbbing of a new-made free-
    man's heart.
In the tyrant's breast has entered a strange fear he does
    not own,
In his midnight dreams he seeth visions of a trampled
    throne,—
In the harvest of the whirlwind he shall reap as he has
    sown.
Brighter beams the radiant promise, all the wide earth
    fills with light,

Freedom's rosy morn is breaking after tyranny's dark
  night,
And the noontide of its splendor soon will burst upon
  the sight.

Lo ! Alas ! the promise darkens,—blood has quenched
  its golden glow,
Plymouth's mound in gloom is shrouded, and her
  watch-fires smoulder low,
While from all the land are rising cries of mourning
  and of woe.
Thus it endeth ! like a comet whirling in its fiery flight
Fades the vision of our glories from the startled
  nations' sight,
And the transient dawn is followed by a deeper,
  darker night.
Once again the aching shackles on the fainting cap-
  tive rust,
And the poor, despairing peasant eats again his
  mouldy crust,
Feels his manhood sink within him, cowers lower in
  the dust.
On his blazoned throne, defiant, sits the tyrant as of
  old ;
Once again his vaulted dungeons their complaining
  victims hold,

And once more the stone of bondage 'gainst the prison
    door is rolled.
Fallen! fallen! black the ruins where our ancient bul-
    warks stood,
Sheathed the blade that once was dripping, gory, in
    defense of good,
Lost the high, heroic prestige of our noble nationhood.
Fallen! fallen! Europe's monarchs clap their hands in
    hellish glee,
And with gloating eyes look downward to our pit of
    infamy,
While the cruel taunt is borne us: "Who will hence-
    forth call you free?"

Dark the night of gloom around us, low our sun of
    hope has waned.
But a cry is loudly ringing: "Blood and tears our
    freedom gained,
Blood and tears shall flow yet freer and that freedom
    be maintained.
We are humbled, but not fallen: still the Lord of
    Hosts we trust;
Traitor hordes are gathered round us, burning with a
    murder lust,
Traitor hands have War's red gauntlet thrown defiant
    in the dust;

We accept the bloody challenge, we will meet them on
  the field,
Right's broad banner floating o'er us, His strong arm
  our only shield,
With our country's life the issue *we* are not the first to
  yield !''

Loud the clash of arms resoundeth, and a million
  marching feet
Stately step are bravely keeping as the stirring war-
  drums beat,
And a million men are seeking for the conflict's fiercest
  heat.
Forth from every teeming valley swift the forming
  legions pour ;
Slaughter's crimson hand is lifted, and around from
  shore to shore
A wide continent is shaking with the awful tread of
  War.

   *   *   *   *   *   *   *

When the stormy waves of battle in the after-days are
  stilled,
Not in vain their blood our heroes on a thousand fields
  have spilled,
For the Promise to us given shall in brightness be ful-
  filled.

March 11, 1864.

THE VICTORY MONTH—JULY, 1863.

'Twas the fairest time of summer, and the hillside and
the plain
Were in beauty spangled over with the fields of ripened
grain,
And the ministers of Ceres stood with open hand again.

In the lowland, on the upland, busy reapers toiled
away,
And the harvest-fields were merry with their voices
glad and gay,
As they worked and sang together through the long,
warm summer day.

Happy children in the meadows tossed the scented hay
about,
Or they gayly chased each other o'er the fields in
playful rout,
While the shaded hills re-echoed their laughter and
their shout.

But a gloom fell on the reapers, and they paused amid
  their toil,
For the Southern breezes bore them mutterings of
  strange turmoil,
And 'twas said that an invader was about to cross their
  soil.

Even as they paused and listened, from the dark Po-
  tomac's shore
Came the awful rush of column, with their fronts of
  war,
And a strange new flag was waving where it never
  waved before.

Then our proudest cities trembled, and the people
  shook with fear,
As the cannon's solemn booming fell upon the startled
  ear,
And the dust-cloud upward rolling told the foe was
  coming near.

Drum and bugle loud were sounding far and wide their
  fierce alarms,
And their warning notes went ringing o'er the villages
  and farms ;
Timid men stood still in terror, and the daring rushed
  to arms.

Onward went the grim invaders, like a wolf that seeks
    its prey,
Till they met our own brave legions pressing forward
    to the fray;
See, they grapple in the battle! God assist the Right
    to-day!

Rose and fell the tide of conflict, till our glorious natal
    day
Saw the host that marched to spoil us shorn of all its
    proud array;
And the broken bands of foemen down the valleys fled
    away.

Then the notes of triumph, swelling o'er the land from
    main to main,
Filled the nation's heart with gladness,—bade it beat
    with hope again;
Hark! a voice from out the distance catches and pro-
    longs the strain!

Spoke the lordly Mississippi: "From my sources to
    the sea,
On the boasted rebel ramparts, stand the soldiers of
    the free,
And the dear old flag is waving where the traitors used
    to be."

From the wilds of far Arkansas, from the hills of Ten-
    nessee,
Rolled the grand, inspiring chorus of this month of
    jubilee,
Till the very air was burdened with the shouts of vic-
    tory.

From her borders, proud Ohio sent her greetings with
    the rest :
" He who dared, with fire and plunder, place his foot
    upon my breast,
I have humbled, and my prison holds the Terror of
    the West."

With our nation's story written on the highest scroll of
    fame,
Sing unto the God of Battles praises to His mighty
    name.
He who watched our fathers over, watches over us the
    same.

MY COUNTRY.

OH! my country! my fair country! blue and smiling
    are thy skies,
O'er many a distant ocean free thy starry banner flies,
And a hundred beauteous cities from thy bosom broad
    uprise;
Mighty forests bend above thee, shining rivers thread
    the plain,
Rolling down and down forever to the dark and toss-
    ing main,
Where thy breezes lift and bear them to their sources
    back again;
Mountain breasts have for thee opened, with their
    hidden stores of gold,
Rainbow showers, in sweet baptism, have descended
    on thy mould,
Thou hast sown, and in thy harvest gathered in a hun-
    dred fold;
From the harbors of Atlantic, where thy commerce
    anchor drops,
Back thy path of empire lengthens, and its proud march
    only stops
Where thy eagles flap their pinions on Pacific's moun-
    tain tops;

In defense of Right and Freedom time has seen thy
    blade drip gory;

Fame is thine; let the wide world search the annals of
    its glory,

Not a prouder one will find than thine own heroic
    story.

Oh! my country! my fair country! blest of nature
    and of Heaven!

May the dark clouds o'er thee lowering soon afar from
    thee be driven!

May thy bitter cup cease flowing and the balm of peace
    be given!

Over every hill and valley, from the curling Mexic wave

To the far shores that the waters of thy brineless oceans
    lave,

May His mighty arm uplifted, as of old, unite and
    save!

Land of noble sires and children of the fearless and
    the free!

Ruthless foes may fierce assail thee, yet thy triumph
    still must be,

And the future holds in waiting some great destiny for
    thee.

THE VIRGINIA HOMESTEAD.

SOFTLY is the river flowing by the old homestead to-
night,
Bright the watching stars are glowing, with a mellow,
old-time light ;
Resting o'er the gliding waters, white the shrouding
vapors lie,
And the distant woods are solemn with the night-bird's
mournful cry.

By the bending trees half hidden, the old mansion-house
is seen ;
O'er its gables climbs the ivy with its graceful wreaths
of green ;
But no smoke curls from the chimney, and no lights
gleam through the panes,
Round, and in the ancient building, desolation's stillness reigns.

Where the fountain once was playing, weed and thorn
have rankly grown,
And along the garden borders, that no caring hand
have known,

Wild grass springs, and briers familiar rudely reach their
    red arms wide,
And the thistle bold is springing where the timid flowers
    have died.

Ragged vines drop from the arbors, and the open court-
    yard gate,
On its hinges damp and rusted, idly hangs its broken
    weight.
Where the red brick wall has fallen, moss and mould
    are thick and gray;
Everywhere the signs are written of the sure work of
    decay.

All without is gloom and sadness; and within the
    lonely hall
Moonbeams, shimmering through the window, stand
    like ghosts along the wall,
While from out the farther corner, where the shadows
    hover thick,
Slow and solemn, slow and solemn, comes the great
    clock's stately tick.

And one sad ear to it listens; every dear one from him
    gone,
Sits an old man in the darkness, as the weary hours
    drag on.

On his hand his brow is resting, down his cheeks the
    tear-drops start,
Lone, despairing, he is weeping in his bitterness of heart.

His was once a happy household; joy a wife's sweet
    presence made,
And three sons to noble manhood grew beneath the
    home trees' shade.
Peace was his, till one red spring-time brought with it
    war's fierce alarms,
And the brothers left the homestead for the clanging
    field of arms.

Soon they joined the rebel banner; one fell early in
    the strife,
And another's footsteps followed the wild music of the
    fife
Till the eagles graced his shoulders; but he wore them
    scarce a day
Ere Antietam's field of slaughter drank his young life's
    blood away.

In a grassy dell they laid him, 'neath September's
    fading leaf,
And the sad tale, told his mother, broke her woman-
    heart with grief.

And the other,—a last letter, that the father's tear-
dimmed eyes
Read with fearing haste this evening, open on the table
lies.

"I am hit at last, dear father; I am cold and faint to-
night,
And in this, my dying moment, I have doubted if
we're right;
I have fought the old flag bravely, but this late reflection came,
And I fear what I've called glory is but blackest crime
and shame.

"Do not blame me: I see clearly, and I love Virginia
still,
But to-night my heart refuses with its old mad hate to
thrill;
When you told me they had wronged her, for her sake
my sword I drew,
But our eyes are blind with passion, and we know not
what we do."

Childless, is the proud man thinking how he loved too
well his State,
As in sackcloth and in ashes he is mourning o'er her
fate;

In the full cup of her sorrow has his sorrow mingled
    in,—
Darkly hast thou sinned, Virginia, and art suffering for
    thy sin !

May, 1864.

BREAK THE NEWS GENTLY.

BREAK the news gently,—
    Charlie is dead,
Bullet and sabre wounds
    On his young head.
Lightly the gory locks
    On his brow press;
Death has one hero more,
    Life has one less.

It was but yesterday
    That he wrote home:
"Look for me, mother dear,
    I will soon come.
Sad you have waiting been
    All these long years;
Let your hopes triumph now
    Over your fears.

" Dark is war's thunder-cloud ;
 Safe from its track
Soon you will, mother dear,
 Welcome me back.
We may now think of home,
 Colonel White says,
For we have yet to serve
 Only two days."

Only two days to serve !
 Two days of strife !
Ah ! in much shorter time
 Bullets take life.
Ere the next sunset flamed
 Lurid and red,
Redder, with mangled brow,
 Charlie lay dead.

Break gently the sad news
 That you impart,
Or you may also break
 A human heart.
Break the news gently,
 Charlie is dead ;
Damp lie the battle-clods
 Over his head.

Charlie, so dutiful,
    Handsome, and brave ;
And has his valor won
    Only a grave ?
Has he been spared so long
    Only for this ?
Must the cruel bullet's touch
    Be his last kiss ?

And the poor, childless one,—
    Long she will wait,
Eagerly, anxiously,
    Home by the gate.
Ah ! who will tell her of
    All she must know ?
Gracious God pity her
    There in her woe !

THEIR GRAVES.

RAISE no mausoleum where
    Our dead braves are sleeping ;
Holds a grateful nation their
    Memory in keeping.

Lay them in the valleys low,
　By the rolling river,
Chanting dirges in its flow
　Ever and forever.

Lay them where the sweetest flowers
　Earliest are springing,
And the birds from sunny bowers
　Music flights are winging.
Lay them where the spring will hide
　Each low mound with grasses,
Where the rose will last have died
　As the winter passes;

On the hillside, by the sea,
　Where they've camped or battled;
Where their cheers rang loud and free,
　Or their cannon rattled.
Let their lonely graves be made
　In some distant wildwood;
Or beneath the home-tree's shade
　Where they played in childhood.

Lay them, in their blue coats dress'd,
　Where their comrades found them,
With the sword upon the breast,
　And the flag around them.

14

Place the knapsack 'neath the head,
   'Tis a downy pillow,
And let grow, above the dead,
   Cypress-tree and willow.

Hew no shaft and lay no stone,
   Raise no sculptured column,
The wide land is all their own,—
   Holy, haunted, solemn.
Let the wild winds o'er them shout,
   And the songsters warble;
Green their fame shall live without
   Monumental marble.

SLAVERY.

THE blackest crime that earth has known!
The foulest sin that hell can own!
A monstrous thing more monstrous grown!

A curse to master and to man!
A blight to all within its span!
To right a foe, to good a ban!

Can human flesh be changed for gold ?
Can human hearts be bought and sold ?
Can Christian men such lucre hold ?

The brute is man's, the man is God's,
The meanest hind that meanly plods
Was never born for servile rods ! ·

How long, O Time, must freedom be
With us the vilest mockery ?
How long must we stand by and see

Our eagles perch with drooping wing,
Our country's right hand withering,
Because of this accursed thing ?

If there is power in Heaven's might,
If day is brighter than the night,
If wrong is wrong, and right is right,
This sin must pass from human sight !

LINCOLN MONUMENT.

YES, let the sacred pile arise
  In memory of our fallen One;
His name should be before men's eyes,
  Familiar as the beaming sun.

Freedom's great cause he well has served,
  And loosened all the painful bands,
And surely he has well deserved
  This little tribute at our hands.

Build up the consecrated stone,
  And bid the marble letters tell,
Of all the martyrs earth hath known
  Few ever proved their faith so well.

Then lay the shaft, though vainly we
  His fame perpetuate by art;
His truest monument will be
  Within a loving people's heart.

AFTER THE WAR.

THE OLD FARMER TO HIS WIFE.

COME out into the sunshine, wife, come out into the
    May,
And let us sit with happy hearts here in the happy
    day.
A year ago we hardly dared to hope the time would
    come
When we our absent boys should see all safe again at
    home.
Though they so long unhurt had stood and fought be-
    fore the foe,
We knew not in what hour on them and us would fall
    the blow;
For in the distant South, beneath the unfamiliar flowers,
Lay neighbors' sons in battle slain, and what should
    keep us ours?
But still they wrote us they were safe,—to hear it made
    us glad;
And though we never could be gay, we were not always
    sad;

But as each spring toward Richmond's walls our men
    were led once more,
And the great triumph that *must* come looked nearer
    than before,
We tried to keep the parents' fear below the patriot's
    pride,
And willing be to have them there upon the righteous
    side.
Ah! those were gloomy days, dear wife; do you re-
    member now
How hard it was to always keep the shadows from your
    brow?
Once, half-way in a fierce campaign, when Harry sent
    us word
That he had now his company and wore a captain's
    sword,
I'm sure to hear it you were proud, and yet you gave a
    sigh,
And said that captains were as like as privates were to
    die;
And when, soon afterwards, we heard John was pro-
    moted too,
You sadly said he might be dead ere this for all we
    knew.
But as the cruel strife went on and left us still our own,
We found that sweet within our breasts a timid hope
    had grown;

Perhaps their precious blood, we thought, our land will
    not require,
But their strong arms above, to aid in quenching trea-
    son's fire ;
And when at last the victory came that we, in faith, so
    long
Had waited for, no wail for them blent with our grate-
    ful song.
Why should it be, while neighbor Brown of his four
    sons lost all,
And neighbor Wilton two of three, that none of ours
    should fall?
But safely to us be restored well as they left, and sound,
Excepting Harry's broken wrist,—the two without a
    wound !
Now, there is Will, I do believe he'd just as lief as not
Bear on his handsome face the mark of rebel blade or
    shot ;
And John says *he* is half ashamed to come out of the war
With both his arms and both his legs and not a single
    scar !
But can we be too thankful, wife, to have them as they
    are ?
You know that while they were away one constant fear
    we shared
Was that, although our children's lives in battle might
    be spared,

Forever crippled one or more might unto us come
    back,

As do so many gallant men who follow glory's
    track.

To give the strong, young limb is hard, even for coun-
    try's sake, —

Thank God ! such sacrifice *our* boys were never called
    to make.

And now they all are here at home ; it seems so strange
    to me

To have them working on the farm just as they used to
    be.

This morning, when I first awoke, I felt so stiff and
    old,

I wondered how much longer I the plow could guide
    and hold,

Forgetting that their younger hands would give my
    own relief,

That I no more need sow the seed and bind the harvest
    sheaf.

Last evening, as John and I were in the corner lot,

He asked, "Who drew this furrow here,—you, father,
    did you not?"

I smiled him "Yes," and well I knew how gay had
    been his laugh

Had either Will or Harry drawn one there so crooked
    half.

He knew the old man's eyes were dim, the old man's
    sight was weak,—

I thought I saw a tear-drop shine a moment on his
    cheek,—

And then he said, "You've worked too hard while we
    have been away,

But now I promise you shall have a long, long holi-
    day."

And I cannot be sorry, wife, that day has come at
    last,

I feel these later years of toil have made me old too
    fast;

Help was so hard to get, you know, that I was oft alone,

And then somehow there always seemed so much that
    must be done,

And weeds would grow so fast around, I got discour-
    aged most;

But better twenty crops of weeds than e'en a skirmish
    lost.

And while a nation was to save and freedom's fight
    unwon,

What boy of ours should wield a hoe if he could bear
    a gun?

But now the weary years are gone; oh! well may we
    rejoice!

The silent walls have heard again each dear, familiar
    voice,

The absent soldier-feet have trod once more the fields
      and hearth,
And ours is now a joyful home if there is one on
      earth.
So, come into the sunshine, wife, come out into the
      May,
And let us sit with happy hearts here in the happy day.

CONTRASTS.

I.

FIVE times we watched the spring-tide pass,
Dropping its violets in the grass,
Bringing to mountain and meadow shore
The same sweet life it had brought before.
As fresh as creation's seventh day
The earth in its new-born beauty lay,
Above us the blue, beneath us the green,
With the bounteous sunshine poured between.
·But what to us were the bloom and light?
Over our hearts gloomed a winter night,
Into our homes a presence had come
And bidden the voice of mirth be dumb;

Out of our homes a presence had gone,—
Fathers and brothers, an army as one,
And ere the last storm blew white from the north
We saw them march to the battle forth,
And the earliest flowers could scarcely bud
Before they were wet with a dew of blood.
And the slow, sad winds swelled up from the south,
Heavy with smoke from the cannon's mouth.

II.

But a glad change came,—no more in fear
We wait while the spring renews the year.
The roll of drums no longer we hear,
The call to arms and the martial tread,
But the peaceful hum of toil instead.
No more to the glowing summer air
The torch of the raider adds its glare.
The autumn comes like a glorious ghost,
But its banners herald no hostile host.
The white tents of winter alone we see
Where those of the soldier used to be.
The frozen earth hears no charging tramp,
No sentry watches the chilly camp.
Oh, if war and its woes we could but say
Have passed forever from earth away !
In the calms of peace sometimes we note
The spiders' webs in the cannon's throat.

Ah ! peace itself, oft as frail as they,
May be in a moment blown away ;
For still the sword guards throne and state,
And the idle batteries grimly wait,
Ready their ruin red to pour
O'er blue sea wave and prosperous shore.
But long, my country, may it be
Ere the burst of battle startle thee.
Till the last, last hope of peace is gone,
Never again be thy good sword drawn ;
But to bloodless victories lead the way,
As the great sun leads the hours of day.
Then the happy nations, bright as they,
Shall step by step toward heaven advance,
Leaving their cruel ignorance
Dim behind, like a dream of night
Rayed across by the morning light.
Then civilization shall indeed
Be a glorious fact,—'tis now a need !

THE NAMELESS GRAVE.

APART from all the rest 'twas made,
　In a neglected corner ;
It looked as if who there was laid
　Had died without a mourner.
No date was on the small red stone
　That had commenced to crumble ;
No line by which it might be known
　Who filled that mound so humble.

Above the other graves was seen
　The marble gleaming whitely ;
This was not even clothed with green,
　But briery and unsightly.
The barren moss had crept across
　In cold, dead gray to hide it ;
No pleasant tree to blow there was,
　No flower to smile beside it.

With difficult and cautious tread
　No certain path led to it ;
'Twas plain no mourner sought that bed
　With frequent tears to dew it.

I left the spot, my spirit sad
　　To think that one could perish,
As that forgotten mortal had,
　　And leave no thing to cherish.

Oh, where is he who would not have,
　　When clay enfolds his coffin,
Some hand to keep alive his grave,
　　Some tongue to name him often ?
Ah ! it is pleasant but to know,
　　When death has sealed our lashes,
Some sparks of memory yet will glow
　　Above our fireless ashes.

When I at last this form resign
　　To be with earth reblended,
Unlike that nameless grave be mine,
　　At least by nature tended.
To bloomless vegetation dull
　　Let not my dust be given,
But to some flower beautiful,
　　Or glad green tree of heaven.

THE OLD MILL.

Go you to Braineton road, and wind
   Where it will lead you down the hill,
And suddenly it ends, you find,
   Before an ancient country mill.
For sixty years its walls have been
   In rain and sunshine growing gray,
And all its roof with moss is green
   As any meadow is in May.
Wide open hangs the dusty door,
   And swings and trembles in the sound
Of noisy wheels that have for more
   Than fifty years the harvest ground,
Through summer's heat, through winter's cold,
As steady as the seasons rolled.

Oh! often I with playmate band,
   In summer days let loose from school,
Have turned aside to come and stand
   And hear the great wheels splashing cool!
And the old miller kind, who knew
   Well what our childish lips would ask,
Sometimes would come and lead us through
   The place when he could leave his task.

A gentle, good old man was he;
    But once we missed his snowy head,
And when we asked where he might be,
    With awe we heard that he was dead.
But round and round, and round and round,
The wheels still whirled with busy sound.

And often now around the mill
    In pleasant hours I love to stray,
For nature chiefly rules there still,
    And has her sweet, unfettered way.
The brook calls gayly from its bed,
    The birds join in with joyous tune,
And the close cedars o'er my head
    A twilight soft make of the noon.
But as my brow, in daytime dreams,
    Against the grassy sod I press,
A voice falls on my ear and seems
    To chide me for my idleness,
As round and round, and round and round,
The wheels are whirled with busy sound.

I linger where the water steals
    Along the alders dark and slow,
To tread with silver feet the wheels,
    Then join its sister floods below.

I watch it through the hazels wild
  Glide in and out like some gay elf,
And like at play a single child,
  I hear it talking to itself.
O'er the brown arches of the bridge
  I hear the happy swallows call;
The robins hopping by the hedge,
  And the old mill above them all,
As round and round, and round and round,
Its wheels are whirled with busy sound.

And when the frosts have touched the hill,
  Until with fire it seems to blaze,
Again I seek the lonely mill,
  Dim standing in the purple haze.
Like wounded birds, the autumn leaves
  The smoky air are falling through,
And in my breast my spirit grieves
  To think that friends are falling too.
For of the merry group that played
  Where yonder wheels revolving sweep,
Five have I seen in darkness laid,
  To take their last, eternal sleep.

And so it is in life, I say;
  Friends one by one around us drop,

15*

And they are gone and we are gray,
  And yet Time's wheels can never stop.
In vain a moment's pause we crave ;
  Still ever, ever turn they must,
Till, rolling swift across the grave,
  They grind our breathless forms to dust.
The world grows old, the frost of years
  Is gathering white upon its head ;
Its children toil in pain and tears,
  Or slumber sweetly with the dead,
While round and round, and round and round,
Time's wheels still turn with ceaseless sound.

ONLY A LITTLE WHILE.

ONLY a little while,—
  A gasp of feeble breath,
A smile, a sigh, and then—
  Death—death !

Only a little while,—
  A few things done and said,
And heart and hand will be
  Dead—dead !

Only a little while,—
 A transient, troubled day,
Then 'neath the coffin lid,
 Clay—clay !

Only a little while,—
 A gleam, a blush of light,
Then, o'er our earthly skies,
 Night—night !

Only a little while,—
 Let us but do our best,
The end of all shall be
 Rest—rest !

Only a little while,—
 And peace will follow strife ;
And we through death shall find
 Life—life !

WORK.

Sit not with folded hands and wait
  For what the day may bring;
Did men more earnest act, then fate
  Were less a dreaded thing.

The coward only is deterred
  By destiny's weak rules;
Chance is a name, and luck a word
  That's known alone to fools.

On fortune's sea think not to swim
  Atop of every wave,
But keep thy life-bark well in trim,
  Be patient and be brave!

For courage is a talisman
  Most potent and most true;
And patience—ask not what she can,
  But what she can *not* do.

The work must be in part thy own
  If thou wouldst wear the crown,
Prayer and fast will not alone
  Suffice to bring it down.

A RHYME OF CHEER.

OH, friends! what works are by us done
  In gloom that are our gaining?
What triumphs have we ever won
  By sighing and complaining?

Why should we, when the tempest shrouds,
  Sit down in vain repining,
Forgetting that, above the clouds,
  The heavens still are shining?

Unthinking that if it were not
  For dark and rainy hours
The sunshine, falling fierce and hot,
  Would wither all the flowers.

It may be sad truth when we say
  That evil times have found us,
But surely night cannot alway
  Its shadows hold around us.

Let us look up, where, bright above,
  Hope's morning star is gleaming,
Cheer each faint heart with words of love,
  And waken from our dreaming.

And let us not anticipate
    Our future cares and sorrows,
But live through dark to-days, and wait
    The dawn of bright to-morrows.

Nor grasp for joys that they may bring
    With eagerness o'erweening,
Remembering that the brightest spring
    May slowest be in greening.

———————

THE WORLD AND I.

THE world and I have been of late
    Content to live and move apart ;
We do not bear each other hate,
    And yet have little love at heart.
We ne'er were friends, and since I told
    · Its pleasure is but pleasant pain,
It has been pleased to call me cold,
    And I, in turn, have called it vain.

The princes of successful trade,
    And fashion's giddy throngs, I see
Pass by, in all their proud parade,
    Nor deign to cast a glance at me.

I do not envy them their gold ;
   Their pomp and glitter scarce could please ;
For, easier won and kept, I hold
   That there are better things than these.

Those who are titled great I hear
   The fickle, noisy crowds applaud ;
Ah me ! they often do, I fear,
   Think more of men and less of God.
With pride the warrior's brow receives
   The laurel wreath ; but I, with pain,
Look only where, upon its leaves,
   A brother's blood has left its stain !

I have ambition in my breast,—
   But it is not for power and fame ;
I walk in silence from the rest,
   And humbly bear my humble name.
I see the sails of navies spread,
   I see the smoke of cities curled ;
But neither is above my head,
   And what am I to all the world ?

I dwell as by a quiet bay :
   I hear the outside billows roar ;
But well I know that never they
   Can break against my peaceful shore.

And if my walls shut in sweet sights
⌃ The world can never hope to see,
And I've no share in its delights,
    Oh, what is all the world to me?

———————

"HOME AND ABROAD."

INSCRIBED TO W. P. T.

THE heart of him who loves to roam
    O'er strange, new lands and stormy brine,
But still keeps tender thoughts of home,
    Is kin to mine.

And him whose great joy is to let
    At his own hearth his wandering end,
Although we never may have met,
    I call my friend.

Thou'st stood where lowly Afric' weeps
    Alone upon her desert sands,
And in the mocking ocean steeps
    Her poor, bound hands.

By river fair, by mount and main,
  Imperial Europe thou hast trod ;
On many a history-haunted plain
  And classic sod.

But whether dust is on thy feet,
  Or they are wet with ocean's foam,
Still mingles with thy song that sweet
  Refrain of home.

Beneath those alien skies to kneel
  At glory's and at beauty's shrine
Is holy pleasure, which to feel
  Was often thine.

But after it had thrilled thy breast,
  Oh, didst thou not with rapture learn
Another joy, worth all the rest,—
  That of return ?

FLOWERS OF PALESTINE.

(Written on seeing a beautiful bouquet of flowers from the Holy
Land.)

FAIR stranger flowers ! I love your bloom and green,
   For ye are children of that sacred sod
Whereon, in time long past, the feet have been
      Of the incarnate God.

And ages after He had drank the cup
   Of earthly woe and joined His cherubim,
Your beauteous forms to life and light sprang up,
      As should our faith in Him.

Ye are our teachers, flowers ! I may not stand
   Upon the shores where your fair sisters blow,
But that rare loveliness is in that land
      By your sweet selves I know.

And, flowers, ye give me faith,—I cannot stand
   Upon the shores of centuries ago,
But that our Christ was then within the land
      By Christian love I know.

DOWN BY THE MILL.

Down by the mill, where the buttercups grew,
Giving the meadows a golden hue,—
Another field of the Cloth of Gold,
Like that in England's history told,—
Oft I wandered when life was new,
Down by the mill, where the buttercups grew.

The little live brook ran rippling by,—
Which was the happiest, it or I?
The breeze, with ceaseless summer sound,
Like an airy river flowed around,
And the happy woods thrilled through and through,
Down by the mill, where the buttercups grew.

Overhead the sky, like a bright blue bay,
Shored by the hill-tops, wound away;
Early the evening shadows fell
Cool across that beautiful dell;
Long on the grass lay the morning dew,
Down by the mill, where the buttercups grew.

Never the hours shall be forgot
That I lived in that lonely and lovely spot.

Oh for a breath of the fragrant air
That I know is softly blowing there !
For a single hour of the peace I knew
Down by the mill, where the buttercups grew !

———————————

THE RUINED HOME.

DULL through the night its windows stare,
    Its hearth is dark and cold ;
It stands forlorn, as if aware
    That it is lone and old.

Like lower stars before it gleam
    The lamps that light the town ;
Above, the moon·in one broad beam
    Looks in cold pity down.

Its roof is clad with heavy snow,
    And through its broken doors
The whitened wind has dared to blow
    And drift the cheerless floors.

Ay, on the spot where once the wave
    Of household light flowed warm,

A snow-drift like a winter grave
  Is moulded by the storm.

Silence would be in every room
  Were not the winds at strife;
They beat about, and make the gloom
  Seem full of ghostly life.

With every movement of the blast
  Old voices call around;
Old forms come thronging from the past,
  Invisible as sound.

But such sweet presence lacks its proof;
  The time was long ago
When summer rain beat on that roof,
  And happy hearts below.

Such once were there, but now they all
  Are dead or far away;
Comfort no more will cheer that hall,
  Nor pleasure make it gay.

Thus all that Death can claim as his
  He follows to destroy,
And, oh! how willing Silence is
  To hush the notes of joy!

How soon the birds that sweetest sing
   Forsake the summer's bowers !
How easily the hand of spring
   Is loosened from her flowers !

How soon the beautiful and bright
   Surrender to decay !
How closely does the black-winged night
   Pursue the flying day !

But never all the world at once
   By darkness is possessed ;
Some half our planet always fronts
   The sky with lighted breast.

Let cheerful hands still plant and build,
   Although their works are frail,
And time to overthrow them skilled,
   For every hill and vale

Must be a desert or a home ;
   Earth has no vacant spot,
And death and loneliness will come
   Where life and love are not.

THE LOST SHIP.

ONCE a vessel left our bay
　　In the morning's beaming ;
Oh ! how proud she moved away,
With her pennon waving gay
　　And her white sails gleaming !

'Twixt us and the sun, each mast
　　Swayed with stately motion,
As, before the west wind, fast
O'er the harbor bar she passed
　　For the southern ocean.

Loudly from her full deck she
　　Sent her farewell cheering,—
Glad that vessel seemed to be
That the rough and open sea
　　She once more was nearing.

From the low coast's highest rise
　　Sailors' wives and daughters
Watched her with their straining eyes,
Till they lost her where the skies
　　Touched the tossing waters.

Thus she left that sun-bright shore,—
　Left it, and forever;
For across the torrid main
To those waiting ones again
　Came that vessel never.

With half-happy, anxious hearts
　They went forth to greet her,
When 'twas time for her to come
From her distant wand'ring home;
　But they did not meet her.

Weary weeks went by while they
　Watched and hoped and waited,
Looking down the peaceful bay,
Peering through the far-away,
　For that ship belated.

Hard it was for wife and maid
　To accept their sorrow.
For awhile they fondly said,
"She has only been delayed;
　She will come to-morrow."

But to-morrow came, and still
　Saw they not her pennon;

List'ning, day by day they stood,
But their quick ears never could
   Hear her signal cannon.

How she perished none could tell;
   For the years, slow gliding,
Of the fate of that good ship
Nothing learned from page or lip,
   Heard·no tale or tiding.

Had she struck a hidden rock?
   Or, with flame and thunder,
Had a hurricane in wrath
Swept her from its fearful path?—
   We could only wonder.

When her brave crew found their graves
   Little has it mattered;
Down beneath the noisy waves,
Somewhere in the ocean caves,
   Their white bones are scattered.

Long within the sailor's cot
   There were tears and sighing;
Now the tale is half forgot,
And in yonder churchyard spot
   Are the mourners lying.

Let us trust that sailor band,
　　Maiden, wife, and mother,—
Those who died by sea and land,—
On some higher, happier strand
　　See again each other.

SILENCED.

A DAY is dark and sad to me;
　　But smiling hope comes softly near
　　And gently whispers in my ear,
" To-morrow shall be bright for thee."

To-morrow comes; I cannot fling
　　My little heart-aches all aside,
　　And so, I say that hope has lied,
And is at best a cheating thing.

Sorrow's pale mists still shroud my morns,
　　And, murmuring to myself, I say:
　　" Sure all along life's weary way
The flowers are fewer than the thorns.

" Our pleasures have their bitter pain,
　　Our triumphs end in our defeat,

Our friendship is but masked deceit,
And our whole life is vain, is vain.''

But shame has voice ; then if I but
    Do count my blessings, not my cares,
    Sweet peace comes to me unawares,—
The wide gate of complaint is shut.

And thus I end with praiseful air
    The lay my lips began with sighs :
    It only needs impartial eyes
To see some goodness everywhere.

"BURY ME IN THE SUNSHINE."

(These were the dying words of the late Archbishop Hughes.)

Bury me in the sunshine ;
    Let the smiling face of day,
And not the shadowy darkness,
    Look last upon my clay.

Bury me in the sunshine ;
    Let no wild tempest frown
Between me and the heavens
    When to rest you lay me down.

Bury me in the sunshine;
  From the blue heights of the skies
Let the daytime's fullest glory
  Beam o'er my sightless eyes.

Bury me in the sunshine;
  I long not for its glow
Because I fear the stillness
  Of the lonely bed below;

But because in life I loved it,
  And I would have it be
Wherever on earth's bosom
  You make a grave for me.

Bury me in the sunshine;
  'Tis the gleam of heaven's dome,
And it will light my spirit
  On its happy journey home.

TEARS.

I.

LONG ago, long ago,
 Ah ! Earth remembers well
From our mourning mother's eyes,
On the dews of Paradise,
 The first tear fell,—
The first of human woe !
 Since then, since then
 From the eyes and hearts of men
How full has been the flow !

II.

Tears of joy, tears of pain,
 Some as sad as on the leaf
Drops the dreary autumn rain,
 With a patient, meek despair ;
 Some like April showers, brief,
When the opening heavens again
 Show even more fair.
 Oh, delicious, balmy grief !

17

A kind of bliss thou art.
   Thy drops destroy no bloom ;
Tears that never outward start, -
But fall inward on the heart,—
   These sear and consume.

III.

Alas ! the tears we see
   Are not the half that fall.
We hide our misery,—
   God only knoweth all.
The face puts on a smile,
Yet all the weary while
   The heart tastes gall.
   We mask our deepest woes,
For bitterer tears are shed
For the living than the dead,
   That no one knows.

IV.

O Earth ! there comes a day
   When a sweet voice from on high
   Shall beam downward through the sky,
Fresh from heaven, and say :
" Weep no more ! weep no more !
   For the living nor the dead ;

Sorrow's long, long night is o'er,
 The last tear shed !''
But how many years,
But how many tears,
 Before those words are said !

THE WEEPING CHILD.

WHY dost thou weep?
What thought has filled thy little breast with pain ?
What hast thou lost that thou didst hope to gain,
 That thou shouldst steep
Thy cheek of rose in sorrow's bitter rain ?

Each curious toy,
That thou once handled with such fond delight,
Lies now uncared for in thy tearful sight.
 Tell me, my boy,
What full-faced woe has put thy peace to flight ?

Within thy breast
Thy heart is fluttering like a prisoned bird ;
Unto its depths thy feelings' fount seems stirred,
 And thou hast pressed
My hand away, with comfort's voice unheard.

Thy trouble draws
Itself still closer to thyself.   Ah, well!
I will not wound a wound and bid thee tell
The secret cause
That, with this sobbing, makes thy bosom swell.

It is not much;
Laughter and shout will soon again be thine;
Thy grief forgot, thou wilt no more repine;
Yet is its touch
On thy young heart like heavier ones on mine.

We are unlike;
That *one* is strong proves not the other so,—
The grief that breaks and has its briny flow
Doth never strike
Deep in the soil its poisoned fangs of woe.

Then weep, my child;
To thee 'tis given to know the balm of tears;
Thy pain is not an inward one that sears,—
Thou hast e'en smiled,
And to thee bright once more the day appears.

THE SUMMER-TIME IS OVER.

I.

THE summer-time is over,—
　It has had its fragrant growth,—
The leaf is on the clover,
　And the snow is on them both.

II.

The winds are southward blowing,
　The sunny days are few,
And the nights, so long in going,
　Bring us frost instead of dew.

III.

But though earth be at its drearest,
　And the outward light depart,
There's *another* summer, dearest,—
　We will keep it in the heart.

17*

FAITH AND LOVE.

It may be, dear one, ere our lives are done
   We shall lose our hearts' sweet mood ;
For it seems to be man's choice to see
   The evil before the good.
The kindest word may be lightly heard,
   The sun of a smile soon set,
But the deed of wrong is remembered long ;
   The sneer is hard to forget.

Let us live in the light and rule by the might
   Of love, for I think we can ;
But come what will, let us keep with us still
   A faith in our fellow-man.
For he whose heart has felt the world's smart
   Till he never can trust again,
Had better be dead, in his cold grave-bed,
   Than along with living men.

THE ANGEL OF SUNSET.

BESIDE the sunset's golden gates
      An angel waits,
As through them every eve the day doth go,
And, ere it treads the silent lands,
      Of it demands
The story of its hours to know;
And, taking then his pen of light,
      With it doth write
(In lines that will undimmed appear
When all that earthly hands have traced
      Shall be effaced)
Whate'er of good or evil he may hear.

And when each glad, each faltering word .
      At last is heard,
And to the deathless pages given,
With smiling or with pitying look
      He shuts the book
And hands the record up to heaven.
Of all that he has written there
      'Tis ours to bear
The glory or the bitter shame;

He is not merciful, but just ;
 Oh, let us trust
In heaven's high court it will not be the same !

NEVER AGAIN.

THE clouds by-and-by will break and fly ;
We shall see the grass where the snow-flakes lie,
 And the hillsides wave with grain ;
But the loving face at the old home door,
And thy fairy form on the old home floor,
 Never again—never again.

The buds will pout and the blossoms come out ;
We shall hear the happy birds singing about,
 And the patter of summer rain ;
But thy gentle footsteps coming near,
And the sweet, sweet voice we used to hear,
 Never again—never again.

We shall feel the glow that the noon-skies throw,
' And the tenderer light that calms us so
 As the tranquil sunsets wane ;
But the hand whose touch was always soft,

And the lips whose kiss was felt so oft,
   Never again—never again.

O'er sea and isle the summer will smile;
And we may, too, for a little while,
   If only to hide our pain ;
But through it all we will think of thee,
And the world will be as it used to be
   Never again—never again.

REST-SONG.

REST thou, rest thou, weary one ;
Yonder comes the wakening sun,
But the morning, bright and blue,
Brings no work for thee to do.
Rest thou, rest thou, weary one,
For thy work on earth is done.

Done, and well done, faithful heart ;
Thine was no neglected part ;
And the world to-day we see
Better is, because of thee.

Rest thou, rest thou, weary one,
All thy work on earth is done.

We have known thee to complain ;
Not of aching hands and brain,
Not of the burden thou didst bear,
But that thou couldst not others' share.
Rest thou, rest thou, weary one,
For thy work on earth is done.

" Rest thou, rest thou," some did say,
E'en while shone thy earthly day.
But to such thy sweet lips said :
" What but that when I am dead ?"
Rest thou, rest thou ; but in heaven
Living rest shall thee be given.

www.ingramcontent.com/pod-product-compliance
Lightning Source LLC
Chambersburg PA
CBHW030835270326
41928CB00007B/1064